100
GREAT LOW-FAT
PASTA SAUCES

MAGGIE RAMSAY

PHOTOGRAPHS BY
ROBIN MATTHEWS

WEIDENFELD
& NICOLSON
LONDON

CONTENTS

INTRODUCTION

Low-fat pasta sauces? Surely pasta was made to welcome cream, cheese, olive oil and butter? What can compare with the comfort of a creamy carbonara sauce, the richness of pesto or the wonderful aroma of garlic sizzling in olive oil or butter? Of course, it would be nutritionally absurd to do without fat altogether, but since so many people these days are trying to cut down on the amount of fat they eat, especially saturated fat, in this book I've tried to emphasize other flavours.

None of the recipes uses more than ½ tablespoon of added oil per person. Meat, oily fish, cheese and nuts do, of course, contain fat but they also contribute valuable protein, vitamins and minerals to a healthy diet. In combination with pasta, and perhaps a side salad, most of these sauces make a complete, satisfying and well-balanced meal.

My suggestions for pasta to go with each sauce do not always conform to 'rules' about matching pasta with sauces – sometimes they just felt right. It's up to you.

More importantly, in some recipes I've stated 'toss with' and in others 'serve on' pasta. Sometimes it's worth combining the pasta with the sauce so it picks up the flavours but on other occasions the pasta is there to provide a background colour or supporting flavour, so mixing them before they land on the plate would be a mistake.

One of the great things I discovered while cooking my way through these 100 dishes was the joy of fat-free washing up: there are no sticky plates and pans to deal with.

So if you're looking for some healthy additions to your repertoire of pasta suppers, I hope you have as much fun cooking with this book as I did writing it.

NOTE: ALL RECIPES IN THIS BOOK SERVE 4   Maggie Ramsay

Left: Avocado Salsa (page 58)

STORECUPBOARD

An Italian delicatessen or well-stocked supermarket should be able to provide most of the ingredients used in this book. You don't need to rush out and buy them all, but the following selection offers some suggestions for your shopping list.

PASTA
Few storecupboards are without dried pasta. A basic selection might include spaghetti (plain and wholewheat), linguine, tagliatelle, vermicelli or capelli d'angelo, conchiglie, orecchiette, farfalle, macaroni, penne, rigatoni and fusilli. Other appealing pasta shapes include casareccie, radiatore, spirali, gnocchetti sardi, fusilli bucati (which can be long or short), the wide ribbons known as pappardelle and the even broader pasta with curled edges called bretelloni or lasagnette.

ANCHOVIES
These are sold preserved in salt or oil; either way you should rinse them to lose excess salt or oil, then pat dry with kitchen paper before use.

CHILLIES
There are various ways to obtain the hot, spicy flavour of chilli. You can use fresh red or green chillies, dried whole chillies, chilli flakes, ground chilli powder (cayenne pepper), Tabasco and other hot pepper sauces (which are often made with vinegar), or the Asian variations such as chilli garlic sauce and sweet chilli sauce. In some recipes it doesn't matter which you use; in others fresh chillies are essential to add a splash of colour as well as flavour.

FROMAGE FRAIS
This can be used to make a light, creamy-tasting sauce but do not expect the rich 'mouth feel' of real cream. Fromage frais is not a direct substitute for cream and curdles over direct heat. Although you can buy 0% fat fromage frais, I find it rather thin. Instead I recommend 8% fat fromage frais, which has well under half the fat of even single cream.

GARLIC
Simmer, bake, roast, use raw or with just a minute or two of cooking. How much you add is really up to you. If a recipe says 2–3 cloves it means 2 large or 3 small cloves.

HERBS
Some dried herbs such as oregano, thyme and bay have their place as seasonings, but to add a vibrant flavour and a splash of colour I use fresh herbs in many sauces.

LEMONS, LIMES, ORANGES
The tang of citrus juice lifts and enlivens sauces; just a squeeze can do the trick. The zest, pared into fine strips, adds flavour and colour.

MIRIN AND SAKE
These are Japanese rice wines: sake is dry, mirin sweetened.

MUSHROOMS
When choosing fresh mushrooms, remember that button and oyster mushrooms will keep their pale colour and are best for pale and fish sauces, while open-cup and shiitake mushrooms will inevitably darken a sauce, which is fine for meat or lentil dishes.

A small pack of dried porcini (cep or *Boletus edulis*) is a good addition to the storecupboard. They will keep for up to a year, and give a wonderful fragrance and intense flavour to mushroom sauces. They need to be soaked in warm water for 30 minutes before use; strain the water and add to the sauce.

MUSTARD
English mustard is rather harsh. I use the milder wholegrain Dijon mustard to perk up the flavour of some sauces.

NUTS
Although these are relatively high in fat, it is mainly of the unsaturated kind and, besides, nuts are packed with vitamins and minerals. In sauces that are otherwise low in fat I have used walnuts, almonds, pistachios and pine nuts to add both flavour and texture.

OILS
All oils are equally high in fat but most vegetable oils have a reasonably low proportion of saturated fat. For general cooking I use either groundnut (peanut) or sunflower oil but you could equally well use rapeseed or another vegetable oil.

Olive: Olive oil is suggested in recipes where the flavour is a feature of the dish. You won't be using much, so all the more reason to buy the best – extra virgin olive oil.

Truffle: Truffle oil is expensive, but you need only a few drops on hot pasta to add an incomparable aroma. Look for it in Italian delicatessens.

Sesame: Sesame oil is inexpensive and available in most supermarkets and Chinese stores; again, you need only a few drops at the last minute.

OLIVES
Jars of green and black olives in brine may be flavoured with garlic or herbs, pitted or unpitted.

PANCETTA
It really is worth going to an Italian delicatessen to get this delicious 'bacon' (unsmoked but cured with salt and spices). Well wrapped, it will keep for three weeks in the refrigerator. You don't need much to give a lovely flavour, and it doesn't collapse into a limp, watery mess like so much supermarket bacon.

PROSCIUTTO
This cured ham, of which Parma ham is one type, is usually sold thinly sliced. Since the fat is clearly visible, you can cut off as much as you want to reduce the fat content of the dish.

SAUCES
Some bottled sauces are excellent time-saving additions to light pasta sauces. These include chilli garlic sauce, hoisin sauce, light soy sauce, Tabasco, tamari (see below), Thai fish sauce (called *nam pla* in Thailand, *nuoc mam* in Vietnam) and Worcestershire sauce.

SPICES
Keep spices in airtight jars in a cool, dark place. Some useful ones are paprika, saffron strands, ground cinnamon and ground cumin. Ground spices soon lose their fragrance, so buy in small quantities and throw away old packets.

TAMARI
This is Japanese soy sauce, brewed without chemical additives or wheat. Used as a seasoning, it complements pasta and all sorts of vegetables. However, it does tend to darken sauces.

TOMATOES
Fresh tomatoes are the archetypal partner for pasta. They must smell good when you buy them, otherwise you are wasting your money: bland, watery or woolly-textured tomatoes will spoil any dish. Plum tomatoes and vine-ripened tomatoes are usually the best choice.

Canned chopped tomatoes are the basis of many a low-fat pasta sauce. But do choose a good Italian brand; cheaper makes tend to be watery.

Passata means sieved, and usually refers to a smooth tomato purée, sold in jars.

Sun-dried tomatoes are sold in packets that last for up to a year.

Tomato purée adds concentrated tomato flavour where you don't need the bulk of tomatoes. Keep a tube in the refrigerator.

YOGHURT
The best sort to use is unsweetened bio yoghurt, which has around 2–3% fat. Choose 'stirred' rather than 'set' yoghurt.

TECHNIQUES

The most important advice is to read a recipe through before you attempt to cook it. It will also save time if you weigh out the

ingredients and do all the preparation in advance, then you can just cook your way through the recipe without stopping.

COOKING PASTA
It is not necessary to add a tablespoon of oil to the boiling water with the pasta 'to prevent sticking'. The main thing is to use a large saucepan and plenty of water. If there is not enough water, the starch from the pasta will create a gluey soup. Bring the water to a steady rolling boil, then add the pasta and a good tablespoon of salt for every 3 litres (5 pints) of water to bring out the flavour of the pasta. Adjust the heat to keep the water boiling steadily. The bubbles of the boiling water, plus an occasional stir, keep the pasta moving so it doesn't have a chance to stick together. Timing varies greatly according to the freshness and shape of the pasta. Fresh angel hair pasta (capelli d'angelo) is done in about a minute, whereas dried wholewheat spaghetti and orecchiette take about 15 minutes. Farfalle seem to take

even longer, because the middle part where the four layers of pasta are squeezed together is still hard when the edges are cooked.

It is important not to overcook pasta – it should have a firm, lively texture and was never meant to lie in a limp, soggy pool on the plate. Test the pasta at least a minute before the shortest time suggested on the pack and keep testing every 30 seconds after that. Fish a piece of pasta out of the boiling water and bite it; as soon as it loses its chalky centre it is ready to drain and serve. The phrase often used is *al dente* ('to the tooth'); in other words it is firm to the bite.

As soon as the pasta is cooked it must be drained in a colander. Shake the colander well to remove excess water, but you don't need to remove every drop; some sauces, particularly if they are thick, can benefit from a little of the pasta cooking water. Quickly toss the pasta with the sauce or transfer it to a warmed serving dish and pour the sauce over.

QUANTITIES
Depending on your appetite and the other dishes in the meal, allow 50–85g/2–3 oz of dried pasta per person (although friends who seem to live on pasta tell me they cook 100g/3½oz per person for a main course pasta dish).

COOKING THE SAUCES
Don't be afraid to add a splash of water if your sauce is too thick, is boiling too rapidly, or looks likely to stick to the pan.

SKINNING AND SEEDING TOMATOES
Remove the stalks. Cut a small 'x' in the base of each tomato and place in a bowl. Pour boiling water over the tomatoes and leave for 10–15 seconds. Tip away the hot water and cover them with cold water, then drain. The skins should peel away easily. Slice the tomatoes in half around the equator and scoop out the seeds with a teaspoon.

ROASTING AND SKINNING PEPPERS
Preheat the oven to its highest setting. Roast the peppers until the skins blacken, about 20 minutes. Put them in a plastic bag, seal and leave until cool enough to handle. Tip the peppers on to a plate and peel off the charred skins, holding them over the plate to collect the delicious juices. Slice in half and scoop out the seeds with a teaspoon.

PREPARING ARTICHOKE BOTTOMS
Choose fresh-looking green or purple-tinged globe artichokes; reject withered, brownish ones. Soak them upside down in a bowl of cold, salted water for an hour. Have a halved lemon ready to rub over the cut surfaces of the artichokes as you work; this prevents them discolouring. Snap off the stalks and pull off the outer leaves. Slice across the top and pull out the central leaves. Finally, scrape out the hairy 'choke' from the centre – a sturdy, thin-edged teaspoon is the best utensil for this.

CLEANING MUSSELS
Mussels can be very gritty, even if they look clean on the outside. The following method removes as much grit as possible: wash the mussels very thoroughly, scrubbing the shells and discarding any broken mussels and any open ones that do not close when tapped. Put the mussels in a large bowl of clean water with a good spoonful of sea salt and swirl them around. Leave them to soak for at least two hours, changing the water at least four or five times. This may sound like a lot of fuss but it's not difficult to do, and when the mussels are clean they are incredibly quick to cook.

CLEANING SQUID
Pull the tentacles away from the body tube, cut off the tentacles just below the eyes and discard any hard parts. Pull out and discard the transparent backbone from inside the body tube. Rinse the squid briefly, then pull off any purplish outer skin (sometimes this will have been done by the fishmonger).

PREPARING KIDNEYS
Remove the fine outer membrane from the kidneys. Cut them in half lengthways and cut out the fatty 'core' (a small pair of scissors is ideal for this). Cut them in half again and put them in a bowl with just enough milk to cover. Leave for 2 hours, then drain and discard the milk.

UTENSILS

You will probably already have many of the utensils listed below. Some are everyday kitchen items; others, though not essential, will help you create pasta sauces quickly and easily. Top of the list is a large saucepan (around 4 litres/7 pints capacity) for cooking the pasta.

LARGE COLANDER
This is essential for draining pasta. Choose a sturdy stainless steel or enamel one with a base, so you can put it in the sink ready to drain the pasta as soon as it's done.

HEAVY-BASED SAUCEPAN AND FRYING PAN
Stainless steel or enamelled cast-iron pans for cooking the sauces need thick bases to spread the heat evenly, helping to prevent ingredients sticking and burning.

WOK
A wok is useful for quick sauces that can be stir-fried over a high heat.

RIDGED CHARGRILLING PAN
Heavy ridged pans can be heated to a high temperature, then brushed lightly with oil to cook meat, fish and vegetables quickly and give them a distinctive chargrilled flavour. If you don't have one, use your regular grill – again, heat it to a high temperature first – and brush the grill rack with oil.

MEASURING SPOONS
A set of international standard spoons is helpful for accurate measuring of oil, spices and other ingredients (everyday tableware and cooking spoons vary in size). Standard sizes are ½ teaspoon (2.5ml), 1 teaspoon (5ml) ½ tablespoon (7.5ml) and 1 tablespoon (15ml).

KITCHEN SCALES
Choose a set with graduations of 25g/1oz or less for accurate weighing of small quantities (larger amounts are less crucial) to get the correct proportions of ingredients. Many people think they don't need scales, but are often amazed at how far out their guesses can be.

MEASURING JUG
A clearly marked heatproof measuring jug is useful for both measuring and mixing liquids.

CHOPPING BOARDS
Wooden or acrylic boards protect your work surfaces, knives and fingers. Avoid the hard, melamine boards: they blunt knives and, worse, may cause them to slip.

MEZZALUNA
This half-moon or rocking chopper is excellent for chopping herbs, garlic, anchovies and other small items, especially if it comes with a concave board.

PESTLE AND MORTAR
Some herb and spice mixtures are best crushed together in a mortar. Choose a heavy stone pestle to make the job as easy as possible.

BLENDER
Puréeing mixtures in a blender or liquidizer gives a smooth sauce; this is essential in a few of the recipes.

FOOD PROCESSOR
Chopping and slicing large quantities of vegetables is easy with a food processor. It can also help to make certain sauces.

RUBBER SPATULA
Invaluable for scraping down the sides of the blender or food processor.

LEMON ZESTER
This handy little tool is far more effective than a regular grater for paring off neat strips of lemon, lime or orange zest to flavour or garnish a dish.

SLOTTED SPOON
Choose a slotted spoon or draining spoon with small holes, to help you lift ingredients out of a liquid sauce.

WOODEN SPAGHETTI SERVER
Long pasta such as spaghetti tends to get tangled into a solid bird's nest in the pan; a spaghetti server helps you separate it into individual portions.

KNIVES, BOWLS, SPOONS AND SPATULAS
Does any kitchen not have these? Ideally there will be two or three of each: knives must be sharp for efficient chopping; toughened glass bowls in different sizes can be used for mixing and storing; long-handled wooden spoons and spatulas are easier on your pans than metal ones.

THE RECIPES

FAST & EASY

What can we have for supper that's quick, easy, based mainly on storecupboard ingredients

with only one or two items to buy fresh, and preferably cooked in one pan?

Here are some answers, to help you feed family and friends.

FISH WITH RED PEPPERS, PINE NUTS AND PARSLEY

Use any firm-fleshed white fish that won't break up in the pan. Swordfish and sea bass both work well. Canned red peppers make this a speedy dish. Alternatively, use four red peppers that you have roasted and skinned (see page 9). Any pasta will do.

450g/1lb fish fillets	400g/14oz can red pimentos, drained
1 tbsp olive oil	and cut into strips
Salt and freshly ground black pepper	4 tbsp pine nuts, lightly toasted
2 garlic cloves, finely chopped	4 tbsp chopped fresh parsley

Brush the fish lightly with the oil, season and set aside.

Heat a heavy-based frying pan until it is very hot. Sear the fish in the hot pan for 1–2 minutes on each side, until just cooked. Remove from the pan and keep warm.

Add the garlic and red pepper strips to the pan and heat through. Add the pine nuts and parsley, season to taste and toss with hot pasta. Serve the fish on top.

GOLDEN ONION AND ANCHOVY

Combining the sweetness of onions and the saltiness of anchovies, this is a satisfying storecupboard dish for anchovy lovers — easy to make for one person with half a can of anchovies. Delicious with orecchiette.

1½ tbsp olive oil	2 x 50g/2oz cans anchovy fillets,
4 onions, thinly sliced	rinsed (see page 7) and chopped
2 garlic cloves, sliced	Freshly ground black pepper

Heat the oil in a heavy-based saucepan over a low heat. Add the onions, stir to coat in the oil, then cover the pan tightly so they cook in their own steam for about 20 minutes, stirring from time to time to prevent sticking.

When the onions are soft, remove the lid, turn up the heat and stir more frequently until they start to turn golden brown. Add the garlic and anchovies and stir to heat through. Season with black pepper, then toss with hot pasta and serve at once.

LAMB AND MINT PESTO

The flavour of fresh mint complements both lamb and peas in this all-in-one dish. Serve with rigatoni.

450g/1lb lean minced lamb	2–3 tbsp finely chopped fresh mint leaves
1 onion, finely chopped	200g/7oz fresh or frozen shelled peas
2–3 tbsp pesto sauce	Salt and freshly ground black pepper

Put the lamb and onion in a heavy-based saucepan and cook over a medium-high heat for 8–10 minutes, stirring to break up the meat.

Add all the remaining ingredients, then cover and simmer for 5–7 minutes, adding a tablespoon or two of the pasta cooking water if necessary. Season to taste and toss with hot pasta.

SCALLOPS AND LIME

Serve this delicately tangy sauce with linguine.

1 lime	1 tbsp light soy sauce
200ml/7fl oz fish stock	2 tsp cornflour, dissolved in 1 tbsp water
12 large scallops	Salt (optional)
1 tsp shredded fresh ginger	

Scrub the lime, then, using a lemon zester, remove the zest in thin strips. Squeeze the lime juice and set aside.

Bring the fish stock to the boil in a saucepan, then reduce the heat to low and poach the scallops in the stock for 1–2 minutes. Using a slotted spoon, lift the scallops on to a warmed plate. Slice each scallop in half horizontally, cover and keep warm.

Add the ginger and soy sauce to the stock and bring to the boil. Remove from the heat, stir in the dissolved cornflour and bring back to the boil to thicken the sauce. Add a little lime juice, then taste the sauce and add more lime, soy sauce or salt as required. Pour the sauce over hot pasta and top with the scallops and lime zest.

SMOKED CHICKEN AND LEEK WITH WHOLEGRAIN MUSTARD

A rich-tasting sauce with a fraction of the fat you'd get if you used cream. If you can't find smoked chicken you could substitute lean smoked ham. Serve with conchiglie or tagliatelle.

300g/11oz leeks (2 small leeks, with as much green as edible), cut into 8cm/3in lengths, then cut into matchsticks
250g/9oz fromage frais

2 tsp cornflour, dissolved in 2 tbsp water
2–3 tsp wholegrain mustard
400g/14oz smoked chicken, cut into chunks
Salt and freshly ground black pepper

Plunge the shredded leeks into a saucepan of boiling water and boil for about 2 minutes or until just tender – do not overcook. Drain thoroughly.

Put the fromage frais into a heavy-based saucepan and stir in the dissolved cornflour and mustard. Add the chicken and leeks and stir over a low heat until heated through. Season to taste and then serve on hot pasta.

TUSCAN CHICKEN LIVER SAUCE

In Tuscany a piquant chicken liver mixture is served on crostini to nibble with drinks before dinner. Try this variation with orecchiette or conchiglie.

1 tbsp olive oil
1 shallot, finely chopped
1 garlic clove, finely chopped
225g/8oz chicken livers, roughly chopped
100ml/3½fl oz dry white wine
1 tsp tomato purée
100ml/3½fl oz hot chicken stock

2 tsp capers, finely chopped
4 anchovy fillets, rinsed (see page 7) and finely chopped
2 tbsp finely chopped fresh parsley, plus extra to garnish
Salt and freshly ground black pepper

Heat the oil in a heavy-based saucepan, add the shallot, garlic and chicken livers and fry over a medium-high heat for 2–3 minutes, stirring frequently, until the livers are browned all over but still moist and pink inside. Add the wine, stir to deglaze the pan, then reduce the heat to low and allow the wine to evaporate slowly, until most of the liquid has disappeared.

Dissolve the tomato purée in the chicken stock and set aside. Mix together the capers, anchovies and parsley and add to the saucepan, with the stock. Heat through and season to taste. Serve on hot pasta, sprinkled with extra parsley.

SCALLOPS WITH SPICED LEEKS

A bed of mildly curried leeks and pasta is the perfect foil for fresh scallops. Serve with tagliatelle.

12 large fresh scallops
1½ tbsp groundnut oil
Salt and freshly ground black pepper
450g/1lb leeks, cut into 8cm/3in lengths, then cut into matchsticks

1 garlic clove, crushed
¾ tsp curry powder
6 tbsp fromage frais

Brush the scallops with ½ tbsp of the oil, season lightly and set aside.

Heat the remaining oil in a heavy-based saucepan. Add the leeks, garlic and curry powder, cover the pan and cook for about 10 minutes, stirring occasionally, until the leeks soften (add a splash or two of water if necessary to prevent sticking). Season to taste.

Heat a heavy-based frying pan until it is very hot. Sear the scallops in the hot pan for about 30 seconds on each side.

Toss the leeks with the fromage frais and hot pasta and serve with the scallops on top.

SMOKED HADDOCK AND SPINACH

Smoked food gives an illusion of richness without added fat. Serve this with penne.

450g/1lb smoked haddock
1 bay leaf
2–3 sprigs of fresh thyme or parsley
250ml/8fl oz milk
250g/9oz fromage frais

2 tsp cornflour, dissolved in 2 tbsp water
2 tsp wholegrain mustard
Freshly ground black pepper
Large handful of young spinach leaves, cut into 1cm/½in strips

Put the haddock in a sauté pan and add the herbs, milk and just enough water to cover the fish. Bring to the boil over a low heat, simmer for 1 minute, then cover the pan and remove from the heat. Leave for 5–10 minutes, then discard the liquid and break the fish into pieces, removing the skin and any bones.

Put the fromage frais into a heavy-based saucepan, mix in the dissolved cornflour and mustard and stir over a low heat until thickened. Stir in the fish and season to taste with black pepper. When the fish is heated through, stir in the spinach and toss with hot pasta.

Right: Smoked Chicken and Leek with Wholegrain Mustard

FENNEL AND PRAWN

If you're concerned to avoid saturated fat, use olive oil, but the fennel tastes even better if cooked in butter. You could use smoked trout instead of the prawns. Serve with tagliatelle or tagliolini.

2 fennel bulbs	*1–2 tbsp lemon juice*
(about 450g/1lb in total)	*Salt and freshly ground black pepper*
1 tbsp olive oil	*2 tbsp snipped chives*
225g/8oz peeled prawns	

Quarter the fennel bulbs, reserving any feathery fronds. Blanch the fennel in a large saucepan of boiling water for 1–2 minutes, then remove with a slotted spoon, reserving the cooking water. Slice the fennel very thinly.

Heat the oil in a heavy-based saucepan and add the fennel. Cover with a well-fitting lid and cook over a low heat for 10–15 minutes, until very tender. Cook the pasta in the reserved fennel water, then drain.

Add the prawns to the fennel, together with lemon juice, salt and pepper to taste. Add the chives and the hot pasta and toss gently. Serve sprinkled with the fennel fronds.

BEEF AND MUSHROOM

The mushrooms give this sauce a full, rich flavour. It takes very little thought or time to make, especially if you've got a food processor to chop the mushrooms. Serve with conchiglie, lumache or pipe rigate.

400g/14oz lean minced beef	*2 tbsp soy sauce*
1 onion, finely chopped	*1 garlic clove, crushed*
450g/1lb mushrooms, finely chopped	*2 tbsp brandy*
400g/14oz can chopped tomatoes	*Salt and freshly ground black pepper*
25g/1oz Parmesan cheese, grated	*2 tbsp chopped fresh parsley*

Put the beef and onion in a heavy-based saucepan, cover and cook over a medium-high heat for 5–7 minutes, stirring to break up the meat. Add all the remaining ingredients except the parsley and simmer, uncovered, for 20–30 minutes.

Taste and add more salt and pepper if needed. Serve on hot pasta, sprinkled with the parsley.

CHARGRILLED SQUID WITH SESAME DRESSING

Both the squid and the dressing can be prepared a few hours in advance for a really quick finish. This makes a dramatic dinner party dish served on black (squid ink) pasta.

450g/1lb squid, cleaned (see page 9)	*2 tsp sesame oil*
1 tsp salt	*1 tbsp sesame seeds, lightly toasted*
Good pinch of cayenne pepper	

FOR THE SESAME DRESSING:

1 tbsp oyster sauce	*½ tbsp groundnut oil*
1 tbsp tamari	*½ tbsp sesame oil*
1 tbsp balsamic vinegar or rice vinegar	

Slit one side of each squid body and score the inner side with parallel lines 1cm/½in apart, then score the other way to give a cross-hatched effect. If the squid are very small you can leave them whole; otherwise cut them into chunks. Keep the tentacles in bunches but trim off any hard parts.

Mix the salt, cayenne and sesame oil together and rub into the squid. Set aside for at least 15 minutes.

Mix all the dressing ingredients together. Heat a grill or chargrilling pan until very hot. Grill the squid for about 1–2 minutes, turning once, until opaque. Toss the hot pasta with the dressing and the toasted sesame seeds and serve at once, topped with the squid.

SQUID PROVENÇALE

A fragrant, simple supper dish that would be good with conchiglie.

2 shallots, finely chopped	*1 bay leaf*
1 tbsp olive oil	*2 tsp dried herbes de Provence*
2 garlic cloves, finely chopped	*400g/14oz squid, sliced into rings*
2 tbsp brandy	*Grated zest of 1 orange*
100ml/3½fl oz dry white wine	*50g/2oz black olives*
400g/14oz can chopped tomatoes	*A handful of fresh basil leaves*
Pinch of cayenne pepper	

Cook the shallots in the olive oil until soft and translucent. Add the garlic and after 20 seconds add the brandy. Stir briefly, then add the wine, tomatoes, cayenne pepper and herbs. Simmer, uncovered, for 20 minutes or until the sauce has thickened.

Add the squid and cook for 2–3 minutes, then stir in the orange zest and olives. Serve on hot pasta, sprinkled with the basil leaves.

Right: Fennel and Prawn

CHILLI BEEF WITH FRESH CORIANDER

Both the chilli garlic sauce and mirin have some sweetness to balance the fieriness of the chilli. Serve with linguine, egg noodles or Southeast Asian rice sticks.

450g/1lb rump steak, cut into thin strips
6 tbsp chilli garlic sauce
4 tbsp mirin (sweet rice wine)
1 tbsp groundnut oil

2 tsp cornflour, dissolved in 2 tbsp water
8–10 spring onions, finely sliced
on the diagonal
A bunch of fresh coriander

Mix the beef with the chilli sauce and mirin and leave to marinate for at least 20 minutes.

Heat the oil in a wok or a large sauté pan. Add the beef and its marinade and cook over a high heat for 2–3 minutes, stirring frequently. Stir in the dissolved cornflour together with about 4 tbsp of the pasta cooking water and cook for about 1 minute, until thickened. Serve on hot pasta, topped with the sliced spring onions and plenty of roughly torn coriander.

ROSEMARY CHICKEN

Fragrant and fast. You'll probably have the basic ingredients in your cupboard, so you can get this chicken supper on the table in less than 30 minutes. Serve with casareccie or spinach tagliatelle.

2 tsp Dijon mustard
1 tsp dried oregano
2 garlic cloves, crushed
Pinch of cayenne pepper
400g/14oz chicken, cubed

A sprig of fresh rosemary
1 tbsp olive oil
150ml/5fl oz dry white wine
250ml/8fl oz chicken stock
2 tsp cornflour, dissolved in 2 tbsp water

Mix the mustard, oregano, garlic and cayenne together to form a paste, then mix with the chicken and tuck in the sprig of rosemary.

Heat the oil in a heavy-based saucepan over a medium-high heat, add the chicken and sauté until sealed all over. Add the wine and stir to loosen the chicken residue from the base of the pan, then add the stock. Cover the pan, reduce the heat and simmer for 10–15 minutes or until the chicken is cooked.

Using a slotted spoon, remove the chicken from the pan and keep warm. Discard the rosemary, then boil the liquid until reduced by about half. Stir in the dissolved cornflour and bring back to the boil. Return the chicken to the sauce, stir through, then serve on hot pasta.

TURKEY, PROSCIUTTO AND SAGE

Many supermarkets now sell minced turkey, making this recipe even easier. Since turkey is so low in fat, you could finish the dish by stirring in a tablespoon of butter for a rich, rounded flavour. Serve with paglia e fieno (mixed yellow and green tagliolini).

400g/14oz uncooked turkey, minced
125g/4oz prosciutto, such as Parma ham,
finely chopped
8 fresh sage leaves, finely chopped,
or 1 tsp dried sage

125ml/4fl oz chicken stock
125ml/4fl oz dry white wine
Salt and freshly ground black pepper

Put all the ingredients into a saucepan, cover and simmer gently for 15 minutes, stirring often to break up the turkey. Check the seasoning, then serve on hot pasta.

PAPRIKA CHICKEN

Serve this simple, warming supper dish with tagliatelle, accompanied by a crisp green salad or green beans.

4 skinless, boneless chicken breasts
1 tbsp paprika
1 tbsp light soy sauce
1 tbsp clear honey

2 tsp cornflour, dissolved in 2 tbsp water
1 tbsp groundnut oil
150ml/5fl oz hot chicken stock
Salt and freshly ground black pepper

Cut the chicken into slivers, roughly 5 x 1cm/2 x ½in. Mix the paprika, soy sauce and honey with the dissolved cornflour, stir in the chicken and leave to marinate for about 15 minutes.

Heat the oil in a wok or large sauté pan. Add the chicken and its marinade and stir-fry for 4–5 minutes, adding the stock gradually to prevent sticking and to make a sauce. Season to taste, then serve on hot pasta.

Right: Chilli Beef with Fresh Coriander

WILTED SPINACH WITH BROAD BEANS AND PANCETTA

Both beautiful and simple, this dish relies on real Italian pancetta that holds its shape and has a good flavour so you need only a small amount. While the bacon is cooking, pull the grey skins off the broad beans to reveal the pure jade green within. Serve with narrow flat pasta such as tagliolini.

300g/11oz broad beans
1/2 tbsp olive oil
200g/7oz pancetta, diced

2–3 garlic cloves, sliced
300g/11oz fresh spinach
Salt and freshly ground black pepper

Boil the broad beans for a few minutes (depending on size), until just tender, not soft. Drain, then rinse in cold water and peel off the skins.

While you are skinning the beans, heat the oil in a large, heavy-based saucepan and cook the pancetta for about 5 minutes. Add the garlic, stir briefly, then add the spinach and stir until just wilted. Add the beans, season to taste and stir to mix, then serve on hot pasta.

DUCK AND HOISIN SAUCE

If you can't resist Peking duck with pancakes, you'll find the flavours you love in this simple sauce. Serve with fine pasta such as capellini, or with farfalle.

1/2 tbsp groundnut oil
1–2 garlic cloves, sliced
2 large duck breasts (about 500g/1lb 2oz in total), skin and fat removed, shredded
6 tbsp hoisin sauce

1 tsp cornflour, dissolved in 2 tbsp water
8–10 spring onions, cut into thin strips
1/2 cucumber, cut into 5cm/2in lengths, then into thin strips

Heat the oil in a wok or a large sauté pan. Add the garlic and duck and cook over a medium-high heat, stirring frequently, for 3–4 minutes.

Mix the hoisin sauce with the dissolved cornflour, add to the pan and cook, stirring, for 1 minute or until thickened. (Add a spoonful or two of water if the sauce is too thick.)

Serve on hot pasta. Serve the spring onions and cucumber in separate bowls, for each person to add to their pasta.

POTATO AND GARLIC WITH CAVIAR

Use skimmed milk to keep the fat content down – or add a tablespoon of butter or cream for a rich finish. Caviar provides a touch of luxury and a colour contrast (although you could use less expensive lumpfish roe). Serve with tomato pasta, as an appetizer.

350g/12oz potatoes, peeled and diced
2 bulbs of garlic, separated into cloves and peeled
400ml/14fl oz milk

Salt and freshly ground black pepper
3–4 tsp caviar
A bunch of fresh chives, snipped

Put the potatoes, garlic and milk in a saucepan and bring to the boil. Cover and simmer for about 15 minutes or until the potatoes are tender. Push the mixture through a sieve or potato ricer into a clean pan, season to taste and reheat gently.

Pour the potato purée over hot pasta, add a spoonful of caviar to each serving and sprinkle with the chives. Serve at once.

SHERRY KIDNEYS

This is one of those recipes that takes longer to read than to cook. Once the kidneys are prepared (which is done two hours in advance), this dish can be cooked in just a few minutes. Serve with tagliatelle.

10–12 fresh lamb's kidneys, cored and soaked in milk (see page 9)
2 tbsp flour, sifted
2 tbsp olive oil
1 garlic clove, chopped

275g/10oz button mushrooms, sliced
150ml/5fl oz amontillado sherry
4 tbsp fromage frais
Salt and freshly ground black pepper
2 tbsp chopped fresh parsley

Drain the kidneys and discard the milk. Pat the kidneys dry and toss in the flour.

Heat half the oil in a saucepan, add the garlic, mushrooms and a splash of water and cook over a medium-high heat until the mushrooms are just tender. Using a slotted spoon, remove the mushrooms from the pan and set aside. Add the kidneys and the remaining oil and fry over a medium-high heat for 3–4 minutes, until browned all over. Remove from the pan and add to the mushrooms.

Pour the sherry into the saucepan and stir over a high heat to loosen the cooking residue from the base of the pan and form a sauce. Remove from the heat, stir in the fromage frais, mushrooms and kidneys and season to taste. Serve at once on hot pasta, sprinkled with the parsley.

Right: Wilted Spinach with Broad Beans and Pancetta

TUNA PIZZAIOLA

A storecupboard meal full of great flavours. It looks especially good made with pimento-stuffed green olives. Serve with penne.

1/2 tbsp olive oil
1 onion, finely chopped
1–2 garlic cloves, finely chopped
2 x 400g/14oz cans chopped tomatoes
6 anchovy fillets, rinsed (see page 7) and chopped

1 tbsp capers, drained
4 tbsp halved pitted green olives
2 x 200 g/7 oz cans tuna in brine, drained
Freshly ground black pepper
2 tbsp chopped fresh parsley

Heat the oil in a heavy-based saucepan, add the onion, then cover the pan and cook over a low heat until soft. Add the garlic, then the tomatoes and simmer for 10 minutes, until slightly thickened.

Stir in the anchovies, capers, olives and tuna and simmer for 2 minutes, or until heated through. Season with black pepper, then toss with hot pasta and serve sprinkled with the parsley.

SALMON TERIYAKI

The Japanese wines give a slightly fuller flavour to the sauce, which seeps into the pasta as you break into the fish. Serve with tagliatelle.

4 salmon steaks or fillets
4 tbsp mirin (sweet rice wine) or sweet white wine
4 tbsp sake (rice wine) or dry sherry

4 tbsp tamari
1 garlic clove, cut into fine slivers
1 tsp vegetable oil

Lay the salmon in a shallow dish. Put the mirin, sake, tamari and garlic into a small saucepan and bring to the boil. Pour over the fish and leave to marinate for 15–20 minutes.

Heat a heavy-based frying pan. Brush the oil over the hot pan, then add the fish and cook for about 2–3 minutes, brushing with some of the marinade. Using a fish slice, turn the fish and brush again with the marinade. Cook for a further 1–2 minutes, or until done to your liking. Serve at once on hot pasta, spooning over a little more of the marinade if you like.

MUSSELS AND SAFFRON

Mussels are cheap, nutritious and, after you've cleaned them, delightfully quick to cook. Serve with linguine.

200ml/7fl oz dry white wine
2kg/4 1/2lb mussels, thoroughly cleaned (see page 9)
2 tsp cornflour, dissolved in 2 tbsp water

Good pinch of saffron strands, mixed with 1 tbsp hot water
125g/4oz fromage frais
2 tbsp finely chopped fresh parsley

Bring the wine to the boil in a very large, heavy-based saucepan over a high heat. Add the mussels and cover the pan. Cook for 1–2 minutes or until the mussels open. Do not overcook them or they will shrink and become tough.

Remove the mussels from the pan using a large slotted spoon (you can take them out of their shells if you prefer).

Strain the liquid into a jug and rinse out the saucepan. Return the liquid to the pan, leaving any grit behind in the jug, and boil until reduced by half. Stir in the dissolved cornflour, bring back to the boil, then remove from the heat and stir in the saffron and its water, the fromage frais and the mussels. Heat through very briefly and then serve on hot pasta, sprinkled with the parsley.

CRAB, LEMON AND PARSLEY

This Italian-inspired recipe is an easy way to 'stretch' a small amount of crab. Serve with linguine or spaghetti.

1 large or 2 small fresh boiled crabs (or dressed crabs)
4 tbsp chopped fresh parsley
Grated zest and juice of 1 lemon

Salt and freshly ground black pepper
A few drops of anchovy essence or Thai fish sauce (optional)
1 tbsp extra virgin olive oil

Remove the meat from the crab and place in a large bowl. Mix in the parsley and most of the lemon zest and juice. Season to taste and, if you like, add more lemon or a little anchovy essence or fish sauce to bring out the flavour of the crab.

Toss the hot pasta with the olive oil, then with the crab mixture and serve at once.

Right: Tuna Pizzaiola

VEGETARIAN SAUCES

All sorts of vegetables go really well with pasta for quick and easy lunch or supper dishes. The combination of pasta and vegetables also makes a good all-in-one side dish or first course, as in the traditional Italian menu.

FRESH TOMATO AND BASIL

This must be made with perfect, full-flavoured tomatoes. Although the sauce is cold, it is traditionally served with very hot spaghetti – use wholewheat spaghetti to feel truly virtuous.

700g/1¹/₂lb tomatoes, skinned, seeded (see page 9) and diced
Salt and freshly ground black pepper
Large handful of torn fresh basil leaves, plus extra to serve
1 tbsp extra virgin olive oil
1 tbsp red wine vinegar

Put the diced tomatoes in a bowl and season well. Gently stir in the basil, then sprinkle with the oil and vinegar. Cover and leave in the refrigerator for 1–2 hours.

To serve, toss the sauce with hot, freshly cooked pasta. Serve at once, sprinkled with some freshly torn basil leaves.

RICH TOMATO AND OREGANO

Deeply tomatoey, this is delicious on its own or as an accompaniment to grilled fish, chicken, lamb or pork. The strips of onion and sun-dried tomato would cling nicely around fusilli.

1 tbsp olive oil
4 large red onions, finely sliced
400g/14oz can chopped tomatoes
25g/1oz sun-dried tomatoes (dried, not preserved in oil), cut into thin strips
2 tbsp chopped fresh oregano
Salt and freshly ground black pepper

Heat the oil in a heavy-based saucepan, add the onions and cover with a well-fitting lid. Cook over a low heat for 15 minutes or so, stirring occasionally to prevent sticking. Remove the lid and cook for a further 10 minutes. Add the canned tomatoes and simmer for 5–10 minutes.

Add the sun-dried tomatoes and oregano and simmer for 5 minutes. Season to taste and toss with hot pasta.

COURGETTE AND MINT

This would make a pretty lunch or side dish, especially if served with fusilli bucati, the open pasta spirals that look like curls of hair.

450g/1lb small courgettes, grated in long strips
1 tbsp salt
175g/6oz shelled fresh or frozen peas
1¹/₂ tbsp olive oil
1 garlic clove, finely chopped
2 tbsp shredded fresh mint leaves

Put the grated courgettes into a colander and sprinkle with the salt. Toss gently and leave for 30–40 minutes.

Rinse the courgettes thoroughly and squeeze dry. Boil the peas until tender, then drain and set aside.

Heat a large saucepan or wok, add the oil, then the garlic and courgettes and toss for 2–3 minutes. Add the peas, mint and hot pasta, toss well and serve at once.

ARTICHOKES WITH SUN-DRIED TOMATOES

Canned artichokes can be transformed into this intriguing sauce in a matter of minutes. Serve with conchiglie or cheese-filled ravioli.

2 x 400g/14oz cans artichokes, drained
3–4 tbsp pesto sauce
1 tbsp olive oil
1 garlic clove, finely chopped
175g/6oz button mushrooms, thinly sliced
Salt and freshly ground black pepper
50g/2oz sun-dried tomatoes, soaked in hot water for 10 minutes, then cut into thin strips
Sprigs of fresh basil, to garnish

Put the artichokes in a saucepan, cover with boiling water and boil for 2 minutes. Drain, then tip into a food processor and purée with the pesto.

In the same pan, heat the oil, then add the garlic, mushrooms, salt and pepper and sauté over medium-high heat for about 3 minutes. Add the artichoke purée and the sun-dried tomatoes and heat through. Serve on hot pasta, garnished with sprigs of basil.

ASPARAGUS, CHERVIL AND LEMON

To make a luxurious sauce without cream you have to work carefully, as yoghurt and fromage frais have a tendency to curdle. This delicate sauce may sound fussy – and it can't be kept hanging around – but it's worth it. Penne echo the shape of the asparagus.

250g/9oz asparagus, trimmed and	*1 tsp wholegrain mustard*
cut into 2.5cm/1in lengths	*Salt and freshly ground black pepper*
2 tsp cornflour, dissolved in 2 tbsp water	*4 tbsp dry white wine*
125g/4oz fromage frais	*Grated zest of 2 lemons*
125g/4oz natural yoghurt	*4 tbsp chopped fresh chervil*

Cook the asparagus in a large pan of boiling water for 2–3 minutes or until tender. Using a slotted spoon, transfer to a colander. Add the pasta to the water and cook until *al dente*.

While the pasta is cooking, mix the dissolved cornflour with the fromage frais, yoghurt, mustard and salt and pepper to taste.

Using a slotted spoon, transfer the pasta to the colander with the asparagus. Pour the cooking water into a measuring jug and return 150ml/5fl oz to the saucepan, together with the wine. Boil until reduced by three-quarters, then remove from the heat and stir in the yoghurt mixture. Stir over a very low heat until it thickens slightly. Add the pasta and asparagus, lemon zest and chervil, heat through gently and serve at once.

Below: Chargrilled Asparagus with Green Olives and Basil

ROASTED VEGETABLE

This combination of vegetables makes a change from the usual Mediterranean mixture. The mushrooms may shrink when roasted but their flavour will be intensified. For best results choose open-cup mushrooms, about 4cm/1½in in diameter. Serve with penne or rigatoni.

1 tbsp olive oil	*350g/12oz mushrooms*
700g/1½lb asparagus, trimmed	*4 tbsp chopped fresh herbs*
of its woody base	*(e.g. parsley, thyme, basil)*
2 red peppers, cut into strips	*Salt and freshly ground black pepper*
2cm/¾in wide	*4 tbsp dry white wine*
200g/7oz courgettes, cut into	
2.5cm/1in chunks	

Preheat the oven to its highest setting. Brush a heavy roasting tin with the oil and spread the vegetables over it. Sprinkle with half the herbs, some salt and pepper and half the wine. Roast for about 20 minutes or until the vegetables are just tender and beginning to blacken.

Remove the tin from the oven and chop the asparagus into 2cm/¾in pieces (you could also chop the other vegetables smaller if you like). Place the roasting tin over a high heat, add the remaining wine and stir to deglaze the tin. Add the hot pasta and the remaining herbs, stir through and serve at once.

ROCKET, GARLIC AND GOAT'S CHEESE

Yes, it sounds like a lot of garlic – but everyone knows that garlic is good for you. The cheese melts satisfyingly into a little of the pasta water to make a sauce for orecchiette or conchiglie.

4 whole garlic bulbs	*Salt and freshly ground black pepper*
1 tbsp olive oil	*100g/3½oz goat's cheese, crumbled*
1 tbsp fresh thyme leaves	*85g/3oz rocket*

Preheat the oven to 220°C/425°F/Gas 7. Separate the garlic into cloves but do not peel them. Put the cloves on a sheet of foil or baking parchment, sprinkle with the oil and pinch the edges of the foil or parchment together to make a well-sealed parcel. Bake for about 25 minutes, until tender.

Pop the garlic out of its skin, sprinkle with the thyme and season to taste.

Cook the pasta and drain, reserving some of the cooking water. Toss the hot pasta with the cheese and 2–3 tbsp of the hot cooking water. Add the rocket and garlic and stir over a low heat until the cheese has melted and the rocket has wilted. Serve at once.

ROASTED TOMATO AND GARLIC

Slow roasting intensifies the flavour of the tomatoes and mellows the garlic. This needs no other accompaniment than green or white tagliatelle, but you could sprinkle on some grated cheese or black olives if you like.

1.5kg/3lb plum tomatoes or
vine-ripened tomatoes
1 tbsp sea salt

8 garlic cloves, unpeeled
1/2 tbsp olive oil

Preheat the oven to 150°C/300°F/Gas 2. Slice the tomatoes in half and place on a baking sheet lined with nonstick baking paper. Sprinkle with the salt and place in the oven.

After 1 hour, add the garlic cloves to a corner of the baking sheet and sprinkle with the olive oil. Roast for a further hour.

Reserve 12 tomato halves. Put the rest in a blender or food processor and add the garlic, popped out of its skin. Blend to a coarse sauce and toss with the hot pasta. Serve with the reserved tomatoes on top.

CHARGRILLED ASPARAGUS WITH GREEN OLIVES AND BASIL

The slightly charred flavour of the grilled asparagus is a good match for the olive mixture. Olives and basil – and even garlic and Parmesan – vary in strength of flavour, so I suggest you begin with the given quantities but have more to hand and be prepared to adjust them according to taste. The olive mixture can be prepared a day ahead, which mellows the flavours. Radiatore pasta would be perfect to trap the little bits of olive paste.

700g/1½lb asparagus, trimmed of
its woody base
2 tsp olive oil
100g/3½oz pitted green olives in brine,
rinsed and patted dry

Large handful of fresh basil leaves
2 garlic cloves, roughly chopped
40g/1½oz Parmesan cheese, shaved
Freshly ground black pepper

Preheat a ridged chargrilling pan or grill to very hot. If your asparagus is really fresh and the stalks are juicy when you snap off the bottom, you can brush it with the olive oil and grill it with no further ado. If you are suspicious about its age, I suggest you plunge it into boiling water for a minute, then drain and grill it.

Put the olives, basil, garlic, Parmesan and pepper into a food processor and process to a coarse purée (stop and scrape the sides of the bowl after 30 seconds, then continue). Taste and add more basil, olives or Parmesan if you like. You could also add a tablespoon of olive oil.

Toss the olive mixture with hot pasta. Cut the asparagus into 5cm/2in lengths and add to the pasta. Serve at once.

Above: Roasted Tomato and Garlic

MUSHROOMS WITH TRUFFLE OIL

Don't worry if you can't get truffle oil – even without it the sauce is still intensely mushroomy. Linguine offers a good pale contrast to the black liquid.

40g/1½oz dried sliced porcini mushrooms
400g/14oz large fresh mushrooms, sliced
2–3 garlic cloves, sliced

2 tbsp tamari
A little truffle oil

Put the dried mushrooms in a jug and add 200ml/7fl oz hot water. Leave to soak for about 30 minutes.

Fish out the mushrooms, squeezing them gently over the jug to collect the liquid. Strain the liquid through kitchen paper into a saucepan. Check the soaked mushrooms for grit, then add them to the saucepan together with the fresh mushrooms, garlic and tamari. Bring to the boil and boil rapidly, stirring gently from time to time, for about 5 minutes, until the mushrooms are tender and the liquid is reduced to a few tablespoons.

Spoon on to hot pasta and sprinkle each serving with a few drops of truffle oil.

LEMON, PINE NUT AND THYME GREMOLATA

This is a delicate and pretty sauce that works best with a small amount of pasta (no more than 175g/6oz for four people) as a first course or side dish. Don't skimp on the lemons – they are a key ingredient, so do buy unwaxed ones and have an extra one ready in case you prefer a stronger lemon flavour. Serve with a fine pasta such as tagliolini or capelli d'angelo.

1 garlic clove, finely chopped
1 tbsp olive oil
2 tbsp pine nuts
2 tbsp lemon juice

Shredded zest of 1 unwaxed lemon
4 tbsp finely chopped fresh parsley
Salt and freshly ground black pepper

FOR THE THYME GREMOLATA:
Shredded zest of 1 unwaxed lemon
1 tbsp fresh thyme leaves

½ garlic clove, finely chopped
Salt and freshly ground black pepper

Mix together the ingredients for the thyme gremolata and set aside.

Cook the garlic in the oil over a low heat for 2–3 minutes. Add the remaining ingredients, then toss with hot pasta and 2 tbsp of the pasta cooking water. Serve at once, sprinkled with the thyme gremolata.

TOMATO MACARONI GRATIN

In a reversal of the usual macaroni cheese, in this recipe macaroni is mixed with a tomato sauce, then topped with cheese. Use a strongly flavoured or mature cheese and you will need only a small amount. It's very filling – allow 300g/11oz macaroni for four people.

½ tbsp olive oil
1 onion, finely chopped
2 garlic cloves, finely chopped
2 tsp dried oregano
2 x 400g/14oz cans chopped tomatoes

Salt and freshly ground black pepper
50g/2oz fresh wholemeal breadcrumbs
50g/2oz Parmesan or mature Cheddar cheese, grated

Preheat the oven to 200°C/400°F/Gas 6.

Heat the oil in a heavy-based saucepan, add the onion, then cover and cook until soft. Add the garlic and half the oregano and stir to bring out the aromas. Add the tomatoes and simmer for 3–4 minutes. Season to taste and mix with the cooked macaroni.

Tip the mixture into an ovenproof dish. Mix the breadcrumbs with the cheese and remaining oregano and sprinkle over the macaroni. Bake for 10–15 minutes, or until the topping is crisp and browned.

SPICED SPINACH AND LENTIL

The inspiration for this dish is Persian. If you really want to go to town, prepare another batch of saffron in hot water and drizzle it over the yoghurt just before serving. Serve with tagliatelle.

50g/2oz green lentils
1 bay leaf
Pinch of vegetable stock powder
250g/9oz fresh spinach
1 tbsp olive oil
1 tsp ground coriander
1 tsp ground cumin

1 tsp finely chopped fresh ginger
1 garlic clove, finely chopped
Salt and freshly ground black pepper
Good pinch of saffron strands,
mixed with 1 tbsp hot water
150g/5oz natural yoghurt
Small bunch of fresh coriander

Put the lentils, bay leaf, stock powder and 500ml/16fl oz water into a saucepan and boil rapidly for 10 minutes, then reduce the heat and simmer for about 20 minutes, until the lentils are tender and have absorbed the liquid.

Meanwhile, wash the spinach and leave to drain.

Heat the oil in a large, wide saucepan, add the coriander and cumin and cook for 1–2 minutes over a low heat. Add the ginger, garlic, salt and pepper and stir for 30 seconds, then add the spinach and stir until wilted and coated in the spices.

Stir the saffron into the lentils, then add to the spinach and stir briefly. Serve on a bed of pasta, topped with the yoghurt and fresh coriander.

Right: Lemon, Pine Nut and Thyme Gremolata

VEGETABLE SPAGHETTI

The secret of this bright and colourful dish is to cut the vegetables into very fine strips so they cook quickly. Serve with linguine.

1 tbsp olive oil	*1 young leek, cut into 8cm/3in lengths,*
1 garlic clove, sliced	*then into thin strips*
5 sprigs of fresh thyme	*4 tbsp dry white wine*
50g/2oz green beans, sliced lengthways	*4 tbsp vegetable stock*
2 young carrots, cut into thin strips	*1–2 tsp balsamic vinegar*
1/2 red and 1/2 yellow pepper,	*Salt and freshly ground black pepper*
cut into thin strips	*2 tbsp pine nuts*

Heat the oil in a large saucepan or wok. Add the garlic and thyme, then the vegetables and stir-fry for 1–2 minutes.

Add the wine and stock and continue cooking over a high heat for 2–3 minutes, until the liquid has reduced to about 2 tbsp (do not overcook or the vegetables will lose their colour). Add balsamic vinegar, salt and pepper to taste and toss with hot pasta. Sprinkle with the pine nuts and serve at once.

Below: Vegetable Spaghetti

CHARGRILLED LEEKS AND RED ONIONS WITH SALSA VERDE

There are many versions of salsa verde, a piquant parsley relish often served with fish. You could use rocket, mint or coriander instead of the basil. Casareccie pasta would go well with this.

450g/1lb thin leeks, trimmed and cleaned	*1 tsp Dijon mustard*
4 red onions	*1 tbsp lemon juice*
Large bunch of fresh parsley, chopped	*2 tbsp extra virgin olive oil*
Handful of fresh basil leaves	*Salt and freshly ground black pepper*
1 garlic clove, crushed	*Lemon zest, to garnish*
1 tbsp capers	

Blanch the leeks in boiling water for 1 minute, then drain and refresh in cold water. Cut the onions in half down through the root end, then cut each half into 3 wedges but do not separate the wedges. Blanch in boiling water for 1–2 minutes, then drain and refresh in cold water. Leave to drain.

Pound the parsley, basil, garlic and capers in a mortar until smooth. Add the mustard and lemon juice and stir well. Using a fork, gradually whisk in the olive oil. Season to taste.

Heat a chargrilling pan or heavy-based frying pan. When it is very hot, brush with olive oil, then add the leeks and separated onion wedges. Grill for 15–20 minutes, turning occasionally, until beginning to blacken all over.

Toss the salsa verde with hot pasta and serve the vegetables on top, garnished with lemon zest.

NOTE

Spring onions are very good chargrilled, and you don't need to blanch them first; try them instead of leeks.

FENNEL AND PECORINO

The sharpness of pecorino cheese contrasts well with the sweetness of the fennel; for a mellower flavour, substitute Parmesan. Serve with conchiglie.

3–4 fennel bulbs	*50g/2oz pecorino cheese, grated*
(about 700g/1 1/2lb in total), quartered	*Salt and freshly ground black pepper*
1 tbsp olive oil	*2 tbsp snipped fresh chives*

Preheat the oven to 230°C/450°F/Gas 8. Blanch the fennel in boiling water for 1–2 minutes, then drain. Chop the fennel quite small and place in a roasting tin with the olive oil. Sprinkle on the cheese, a little salt and plenty of pepper. Roast for 20–30 minutes, until the cheese begins to turn golden brown.

Toss with hot pasta and serve garnished with the chives.

MUSHROOM, SPINACH AND RICOTTA

A vivid green sauce, full of rich flavour. Serve with farfalle

1 tbsp olive oil
2 garlic cloves, crushed
225g/8oz button mushrooms, sliced
Salt and freshly ground black pepper

500g/1lb 2oz fresh spinach, washed,
or 250g/9oz frozen spinach
Freshly grated nutmeg
125g/4oz ricotta cheese

Heat the oil in a heavy-based saucepan, add the garlic, mushrooms and seasoning and sauté until softened, adding a splash of water if the mushrooms seem too dry. Lift out with a slotted spoon and set aside.

Add the spinach to the pan, season with salt, pepper and nutmeg and cook until wilted (if fresh) or thawed (if frozen). Tip the spinach and any liquid into a food processor or blender, add the ricotta and purée until smooth.

Return the mushrooms to the pan, add the spinach sauce and heat through gently. Toss with hot pasta.

SWEET POTATO AND BROCCOLI

Try to get the golden-fleshed sweet potatoes for this dish: the white-fleshed ones tend to be rather mealy textured. Serve with spirali or rigatoni.

350g/12oz sweet potatoes, quartered
250g/9oz broccoli, cut into small florets
1 tbsp olive oil
1 garlic clove, finely chopped
1 tbsp finely chopped fresh ginger
6 spring onions, cut diagonally into
2.5cm/1in lengths

1 tbsp light soy sauce
200ml/7fl oz tomato passata
Small handful of fresh basil leaves,
roughly torn
Salt and freshly ground black pepper

Boil the sweet potatoes until just tender. Drain, refresh in cold water, then peel off the skins. Cut the potatoes into 2cm/¾in chunks. Boil the broccoli until just tender, drain and refresh.

Heat the oil in a wok or large, heavy-based sauté pan, add the garlic, ginger and spring onions and stir-fry for 30 seconds. Add the broccoli and sweet potatoes and stir-fry for 2–3 minutes. Add the soy sauce, stir briefly, then add the passata and basil and bring to the boil. Season to taste, toss with hot pasta and serve at once.

Above: Roasted Pumpkin and Sage

ROASTED PUMPKIN AND SAGE

The bright orange cubes of pumpkin are set against a background of tomatoes, sage and onion that is picked up by the pasta. This would be good with spaghetti or casareccie.

1 small pumpkin or butternut squash
(about 700g/1½lb), peeled, seeded
and cut into 1cm/½in chunks
1 onion, chopped
4 tomatoes, skinned, seeded
(see page 9) and diced

Bunch of fresh sage leaves
1 tbsp olive oil
4 tbsp dry white wine
Salt and freshly ground black pepper

Preheat the oven to 230°C/450°F/Gas 8. Spread the pumpkin, onion and tomatoes out in a heavy roasting tin and tuck 4–6 large sage leaves or sprigs of sage among them. Drizzle with the olive oil, then roast for about 20 minutes, until the pumpkin is tender. Meanwhile, finely chop some more sage leaves (you will need about 1 tablespoon).

Remove the roasting tin from the oven, add the wine and chopped sage and place over a medium heat for about 1 minute, stirring to deglaze the tin. Season to taste. Remove from the heat, add the hot pasta and stir briefly to coat it in the sauce. Serve at once.

HOT & SPICY SAUCES

Pasta makes the perfect background to hot chilli or ginger sauces – think of all the classic Asian dishes served with noodles.

Some varieties of chilli are very hot, others quite mild, and unless you are a chilli fanatic it can be difficult to judge the right quantity.

I suggest you begin with a small amount, then taste the sauce – you can always add more.

BROCCOLI AND HOT RED PEPPER

Inspired by the Spanish romesco sauce, this version is lighter than the original, which uses olive oil and fried bread. Serve with almost any pasta shape.

3 red peppers
3 tomatoes
2 garlic cloves, roughly chopped
Dash or two of Tabasco sauce

Salt and freshly ground black pepper
450g/1lb broccoli
15g/¹/₂oz flaked almonds, lightly toasted

Preheat the oven to its highest setting. Put the peppers on a baking sheet and roast for 15 minutes or until partly blackened. Turn the peppers round, add the tomatoes and roast for a further 15 minutes. Skin the peppers and the tomatoes (see page 9). Purée the peppers and tomatoes (and any juices) with the garlic in a blender or food processor and season to taste with Tabasco, salt and pepper.

Steam or boil the broccoli and drain well. Put it on a bed of hot pasta, and pour the sauce over the top. Sprinkle with the almonds and serve at once.

BLACK BEAN AND TOMATO

This fusion of Chinese flavourings with tomatoes would be great with fusilli, especially the bright yellow corn fusilli sold in some supermarkets and healthfood stores. Look for preserved black beans in Chinese food shops.

3 tbsp salted and fermented black beans
2 tbsp rice wine, dry sherry or vermouth
1 tbsp olive oil
2 large garlic cloves, finely chopped
1¹/₂ tbsp finely chopped fresh ginger

Bunch of spring onions
(white and green parts), chopped
175g/6oz sweetcorn kernels
2 x 400g/14oz cans chopped tomatoes
2 tbsp light soy sauce

Soak the black beans in the rice wine or sherry while you prepare the remaining ingredients.

Heat the oil in a large saucepan or wok. Add the garlic, ginger and half the spring onions and stir-fry for 1 minute. Add the black beans and sweetcorn, stir for a few seconds, then add the tomatoes and soy sauce and heat through. Serve on hot pasta, sprinkled with the remaining spring onions.

ROASTED CORN AND COURGETTE SALSA

This bright and busy vegetarian sauce could be served with pasta shells to entrap the corn kernels. Invest in a fresh pack of ground cumin – the brown dust that's been in your cupboard for months will do nothing for this dish.

2 corn cobs
450g/1lb courgettes, cut into
5cm/2in chunks
1 tbsp olive oil
1 tbsp ground cumin
Salt and freshly ground black pepper

1 fresh red chilli, finely chopped
2 tbsp chopped fresh coriander
1 tbsp fresh lime juice
4 ripe tomatoes, skinned, seeded
(see page 9) and diced
4 spring onions, thinly sliced

Preheat the oven to 200°C/400°F/Gas 6. Place the corn cobs and courgette chunks on a baking sheet, brush lightly with the oil and sprinkle with the cumin, salt and pepper. Roast, turning occasionally, until tender and beginning to brown, about 25–30 minutes. Leave until cool enough to handle.

Cut the courgette chunks in half, then in half again to make half-moon-shaped chunks. Hold the corn cobs upright on a chopping board and use a knife to scrape off the kernels.

Mix the corn and courgettes with the chilli, coriander, lime juice and diced tomatoes. Season to taste and serve on hot pasta, sprinkled with the spring onions.

FIVE-SPICE LAMB

A simple Chinese-style dish that would go well with penne or Chinese egg noodles.

2 tsp cornflour, dissolved in 2 tbsp water	1 garlic clove, finely chopped
1 tbsp dry sherry	2 tbsp finely chopped fresh ginger
2 tbsp soy sauce	1 fresh red chilli, finely chopped
1 tsp Chinese five-spice powder	2 bunches of spring onions, sliced on the
1 tsp sugar or honey	diagonal into 5cm/2in lengths
450g/1lb lean lamb, cut into thin strips	2 peppers (red, green or yellow),
1 tbsp groundnut oil	cut into strips 1cm/½in wide

Mix the dissolved cornflour with the sherry, soy sauce, five-spice powder and sugar or honey. Stir in the lamb and leave to marinate while you prepare the remaining ingredients.

Heat the oil in a wok, add the garlic, ginger and chilli and stir-fry for 1 minute. Add the lamb and its marinade and stir-fry for 2–3 minutes, until the lamb is browned. Add the spring onions and peppers and stir-fry for 2–3 minutes, adding a little water if necessary to prevent sticking. Serve at once on hot pasta.

NOTE
Chump steaks, trimmed of their fat and sliced, are wonderfully tender when stir-fried.

Below: Baby Onion Curry

BABY ONION CURRY

Use the smallest onions you can find – or use shallots, which often divide themselves in half when you peel them. Pappardelle or tagliatelle would be a calm background to the hot, busy sauce.

4 tbsp sultanas	2 tbsp mild curry paste
200ml/7fl oz sweet white wine	Good pinch of turmeric
(e.g. a Bordeaux such as Loupiac	250ml/8fl oz vegetable stock
or Monbazillac)	1 tbsp mango chutney (just the liquid)
20–24 baby onions or shallots	4 tbsp natural yoghurt
(about 400g/14oz)	1 dessert apple, peeled, cored and diced
2 largish carrots (about 200g/7oz),	2 tbsp roughly chopped fresh coriander
cut into matchsticks	
1 largish leek (about 200g/7oz),	
thinly sliced	

Soak the sultanas in 2 tbsp of the wine. Meanwhile, blanch the onions or shallots in boiling water for 1–2 minutes. Drain and refresh in cold water, then peel and place in a small, heavy-based saucepan (just large enough to hold them in a single layer) with the remaining wine. Cover the pan, place over a low heat and simmer gently, shaking the pan occasionally, until the onions are tender when pierced with a skewer. Remove the lid and turn the heat up to medium-high, so the wine evaporates and the onions become golden brown.

Meanwhile, blanch the carrots in boiling water for 1 minute. Drain, refresh and set aside.

Put the leek, curry paste, turmeric and stock in a saucepan, cover and simmer for 8–10 minutes, until the leek is tender. Purée in a food processor until smooth. Add the mango chutney and yoghurt and purée briefly, then return to the cleaned saucepan.

Add the apple, the sultanas and their soaking liquid and the blanched carrots and heat through. Season to taste and serve on hot pasta, topped with the glazed onions and coriander.

ANCHOVY AND BROCCOLI

In the traditional version of this dish – from Apulia in southern Italy – the anchovies are blended into a rich, oily sauce. Here, using very little oil, they still make a delicious sauce for the broccoli and orecchiette or pasta shells.

450g/1lb broccoli, cut into small florets, stalks sliced into thin 'coins'
1 tbsp olive oil
2 garlic cloves, sliced
50g/2oz can anchovy fillets, rinsed (see page 7) and chopped

1/2 fresh red chilli, finely chopped
Freshly ground black pepper
A few drops of chilli oil (optional)

Cook the broccoli in boiling water for 2–3 minutes, then drain and set aside.

Heat the oil in a saucepan over a low heat, add the garlic and anchovies and cook for 2–3 minutes, mashing the anchovies so they form a paste. Add the chilli and 4 tbsp of the pasta cooking water and stir well. Add the broccoli and plenty of black pepper, then add the hot pasta and mix well. If you like, finish by sprinkling on a few drops of chilli oil.

MUSSEL MASALA

Mussels have quite a strong flavour so they are more than a match for a curry sauce. Try this with tagliatelle.

1 tbsp groundnut oil
1 onion, finely chopped
1 garlic clove, crushed
2 tbsp curry paste

2 kg/4 1/2lb mussels, thoroughly cleaned (see page 9)
4 tbsp natural yoghurt
2 tbsp chopped fresh coriander

Heat the oil in a very large, heavy-based saucepan, add the onion and garlic and cook until softened. Add the curry paste and cook for 1 minute, then add the mussels, turn up the heat and cover the pan. Cook for 1–2 minutes or until the mussels open. Do not overcook them or they will shrink and become tough.

Take the mussels out of the pan with a large slotted spoon and remove them from their shells.

Meanwhile, return the saucepan to the heat and add the yoghurt. Boil until reduced and thickened (the yoghurt will curdle, but it doesn't matter in this sauce). Remove from the heat, return the mussels to the sauce, then serve on hot pasta, sprinkled with the coriander.

Above: Anchovy and Broccoli

DUCK AND MANGO

The flavours here are not so much hot as bright and lively, with ginger and lime. Serve with penne.

1/2 tbsp groundnut oil
2 large duck breasts (about 500g/1lb 2oz in total), skin and fat removed, cut into thin strips
2 tbsp shredded fresh ginger
1 tbsp honey

Grated zest of 2 limes
2 tbsp lime juice
1 mango, peeled, stoned and sliced into matchsticks
10–12 spring onions, finely sliced on the diagonal
Salt and freshly ground black pepper

Heat a large, wide saucepan or a wok over a high heat, add the oil and duck and stir-fry for 3–4 minutes. Add all the remaining ingredients and stir-fry for a further 1–3 minutes, until heated through. Season to taste and toss with hot pasta.

MOROCCAN SPICED AUBERGINE

The spices in this vegetarian dish are quite gentle. Serve with rigatoni or spirali.

1 aubergine, cut into 1cm/¹/2in cubes
Salt and freshly ground black pepper
2 tbsp vegetable oil
1 onion, finely chopped
2 tsp paprika
¹/2 tsp ground cumin
¹/4 tsp ground allspice
¹/4 tsp ground cinnamon
2 garlic cloves, finely chopped

Pinch of sugar
Good pinch of saffron strands, mixed with 1 tbsp hot water
1 small red and 1 small yellow pepper, cut into 2cm/³/4in dice
2–3 tbsp lemon juice
4–6 tbsp orange juice
2 tbsp torn fresh basil leaves

Put the aubergine cubes in a colander and sprinkle with plenty of salt. Leave for 20–30 minutes. Rinse the aubergine well, then return to the colander or place in a steamer. Cover and steam over boiling water for about 15–20 minutes, until tender, stirring once.

Meanwhile, heat the oil in a heavy-based saucepan, add the onion and spices and cook over a medium heat, stirring constantly, for about 2 minutes, until fragrant. Add the garlic, sugar, about 200ml/7fl oz water and some salt and pepper to taste. Cover and simmer gently for about 20 minutes, stirring occasionally.

Add the steamed aubergine, saffron water, peppers, 2 tbsp lemon juice and 4 tbsp orange juice. Simmer, uncovered, for 5–8 minutes. Taste and add more sugar, lemon or orange juice, salt or pepper as necessary. Stir in the basil, then serve on hot pasta.

TOMATO CURRY SAUCE WITH SMOKED TOFU

This is a vegetarian dish but you could replace the smoked tofu with prawns or mussels. Serve with fusilli or another pasta with curves to hold the sauce.

1 tbsp groundnut oil
2 tsp black mustard seeds
1 leek, finely sliced
4 tomatoes, skinned (see page 9) and chopped
1 red pepper, roughly chopped

1 tsp curry powder
2 tbsp basmati rice
175ml/6fl oz milk
175ml/6fl oz water
Salt and freshly ground black pepper
200g/7oz smoked tofu, cubed

Heat the oil in a heavy-based saucepan, add the mustard seeds and then as soon as they begin to crackle add the leek. Turn the leek in the oil for 2 minutes, then add all the remaining ingredients except the tofu. Bring to the boil and simmer for about 20 minutes, until the rice is very tender.

Purée in a blender or food processor until smooth and season to taste. Return to the saucepan, add the tofu and simmer for 5 minutes, until heated through. Serve on hot pasta.

Right: Moroccan Spiced Aubergine

HOT PRAWNS WITH BASIL

Simple, delicious and versatile, this can be made with cooked or uncooked prawns, fresh or dried chilli or Tabasco sauce, and just about any type of pasta.

5cm/2in piece of fresh ginger,
roughly chopped
2 garlic cloves, chopped
1 tsp salt
1 tsp sugar
2 tsp vinegar

1 tbsp vegetable oil
300g/11oz prawns
1 small red chilli, finely sliced,
or a dash or two of Tabasco sauce
4 tbsp shredded fresh basil leaves

Using a pestle and mortar or a spice grinder, blend together the ginger, garlic, salt, sugar, vinegar and oil. Heat a wide saucepan or wok and cook the spice paste over a low heat for about 2 minutes, stirring occasionally.

Add the prawns, chilli or Tabasco and shredded basil and cook for a further 2–3 minutes, until the prawns are cooked or heated through. Serve on hot pasta.

Below: *Hot Prawns with Basil*

CRAB, GINGER AND BABY CORN

Salty, sweet and citrus flavours come together in this colourful dish inspired by a Thai salad. I have kept the flavours fairly mild but let your tastebuds tell you whether to add more ginger, chilli, lemongrass or lime. Tagliatelle would be my preferred pasta.

1 tbsp groundnut oil
2 tbsp finely chopped fresh ginger
2 garlic cloves, finely chopped
1 fresh red chilli, finely chopped
2 lemongrass stalks, peeled and
finely chopped
200g/7oz baby corn, sliced diagonally
if large

200g/7oz mangetout, sliced diagonally
2 freshly prepared crabs (which should give
about 275g/10oz crab meat)
2 tbsp light soy sauce
Juice of 1/2–1 lime
2 tbsp chopped fresh coriander

Heat the oil in a wok or large saucepan, add the ginger, garlic, chilli and lemongrass and stir-fry for 1 minute. Add the corn and mangetout and stir-fry for 2–3 minutes. Add the crab meat, soy sauce and lime juice and toss over high heat for about 1 minute.

Stir in the hot pasta and serve at once, topped with the coriander.

SQUID WITH LEMONGRASS

This Thai-style dish would be good with fine vermicelli noodles or tagliatelle.

600g/1¼lb whole squid or
450g/1lb cleaned squid
Juice of 1½ limes
2 tbsp Thai fish sauce
1 tbsp light soy sauce
2 garlic cloves, crushed

2 tsp soft brown sugar
1 large lemongrass stalk, peeled
and finely chopped
1 small dried chilli, crushed
1 tbsp groundnut oil
A handful of chopped fresh coriander

Clean the squid if using whole squid (see page 9). Score the bodies lightly on both sides and cut into pieces about 2.5cm/1in square. Mix together all the remaining ingredients except the oil and coriander, add the squid and leave to marinate in a ceramic, glass or other non-reactive bowl for 20–30 minutes.

Heat a wok or a large saucepan. When it is very hot, add the oil and the squid with its marinade and stir-fry for about 1 minute, until the squid is just cooked through. Serve at once on hot pasta, sprinkled with the coriander.

CHILLI CHICKEN WITH CHICKPEAS

Tomatoes, ginger and cumin go together surprisingly well. Chickpeas may sound an unnecessarily heavy addition to a pasta dish but there are several precedents in traditional Italian cookery. Serve with macaroni.

1 tbsp groundnut oil	*¹/₂ tsp cayenne pepper*
450g/1lb chicken, cubed	*400g/14oz can chopped tomatoes*
3 garlic cloves, crushed	*¹/₂ x 400g/14oz can chickpeas, drained*
2 tbsp finely chopped fresh ginger	*Salt and freshly ground black pepper*
2 tsp ground cumin	

Heat the oil in a heavy-based saucepan over a medium-high heat, add the chicken and quickly seal all over. Remove the chicken with a slotted spoon and set aside.

Add the garlic, ginger, cumin, cayenne and a spoonful or two of water, stirring to loosen the chicken residue from the base of the pan. Add the tomatoes and bring to simmering point, then return the chicken to the pan, cover and simmer for 10–15 minutes.

Add the chickpeas and simmer for 5 minutes. Season to taste and serve on hot pasta.

PORK, PINEAPPLE AND CORIANDER

An easy dish with lively, fruity flavours. Serve with fine pasta such as tagliolini or vermicelli.

400g/14oz lean minced pork	*125ml/4fl oz tomato passata*
1 onion, finely chopped	*175g/6oz pineapple (fresh or canned in*
1 garlic clove, crushed	*natural juice), cut into 2cm/³/4in chunks*
1 tbsp finely chopped fresh ginger	*Juice of ¹/₂ lime*
1–2 fresh red chillies, cut into fine rings	*4 tbsp chopped fresh coriander*
2 tbsp soy sauce	*Salt and freshly ground black pepper*

Put the pork and onion in a saucepan, cover and cook over a medium-high heat for 5–7 minutes, stirring occasionally to break up the meat. Add the garlic, ginger, chilli, soy sauce and passata, cover and simmer gently for 20–25 minutes.

Add the pineapple and heat through for 2–3 minutes, then add the lime juice and coriander, plus more soy sauce or salt and pepper to taste. Serve on hot pasta.

Above: *Clams with White Wine, Garlic and Chilli*

CLAMS WITH WHITE WINE, GARLIC AND CHILLI

Make this classic dish milder or hotter by using less or more chilli. Serve with spaghetti.

1kg/2¹/4lb clams in their shells	*1–2 fresh red chillies, finely chopped*
150ml/5fl oz dry white wine	*4 tbsp finely chopped fresh parsley*
1 tbsp olive oil	*Freshly ground black pepper*
2 garlic cloves, finely chopped	

Soak the clams in cold water for 1 hour, then wash them well.

Bring the wine to the boil in a saucepan, add the clams, cover the pan and boil until the shells open, about 2 minutes (you may need to do this in 2 batches).

Using a slotted spoon, transfer the clams to a colander. Boil the liquid in the pan until reduced by half, then strain into a jug, leaving behind any grit.

Clean the saucepan and add the olive oil, garlic, chilli and parsley. As soon as they start to sizzle and become fragrant, add the clams, the strained cooking liquid and the hot spaghetti. Season with black pepper, stir gently to mix well, then serve at once.

SUBSTANTIAL SAUCES

When pasta takes centre stage, it's easy to upgrade it to luxury class. As the following low-fat recipes show,

you don't need to add cream to make a pasta dish that's fit for any feast.

SALMON WITH SOY, MUSTARD AND DILL

If you're a fan of gravad lax, this is the sauce for you. Serve on fresh tagliatelle.

2¹/₂ tbsp cider vinegar
3 tbsp wholegrain mustard
2 tbsp soft brown sugar
2 tbsp vegetable oil

Salt and freshly ground black pepper
450g/1lb salmon fillet, skinned and boned
2 tbsp tamari
3–4 tbsp chopped fresh dill

Mix together the vinegar, mustard and sugar. Whisk in the oil and season to taste.

Cut the salmon into strips 2.5cm/1in wide and toss with the tamari and 1 tbsp of the mustard mixture. Cook in a hot wok or heavy-based frying pan for a minute or two; do not overcook or the salmon will break up.

Add the dill to the remaining mustard mixture, toss with the salmon, and serve at once, on a bed of hot pasta.

WHITE BEAN AND ROSEMARY WITH TRUFFLE OIL

Truffle oil is worth the extravagance – it lasts for ages and it really does elevate the humble bean to great heights. Serve with farfalle.

400g/14oz can cannellini or
haricot beans, drained and rinsed
300ml/10fl oz well-flavoured
vegetable stock

2 sprigs of fresh rosemary
1–2 tsp truffle oil
Salt and freshly ground black pepper
1 tbsp snipped fresh chives

Put the beans in a saucepan with the stock and rosemary. Cover and simmer for 10 minutes.

Remove the rosemary. In a blender or food processor, purée the stock with about two-thirds of the beans and 1 tsp of the truffle oil. Return to the saucepan and heat through, then season to taste and pour over hot pasta. Sprinkle a few drops of truffle oil, some freshly ground black pepper and the chives over the pasta and serve at once.

MUSSELS, FENNEL AND PERNOD

The combination of mussels and fennel is quite delicious, and a splash of Pernod accentuates both ingredients. Serve with orecchiette or conchiglie.

1 tbsp olive oil
2 fennel bulbs, finely chopped
1 garlic clove, crushed
¹/₂ lemon

1 tbsp Pernod
2 kg/4¹/₂lb mussels, cleaned (see page 9)
2 tbsp chopped fresh parsley
1 tbsp chopped fresh dill

Heat the oil in a very large, heavy-based saucepan. Add the fennel and garlic and cook over a low heat until softened. Add a squeeze of lemon juice, then the Pernod and the mussels, turn up the heat and cover the pan. Cook for 1–2 minutes or until the mussels open. Do not overcook them or they will shrink and become tough.

Serve on hot pasta, sprinkled with the parsley and dill.

CAJUN CHICKEN

You should have most of the ingredients for this spicy dish in your cupboard – it's just a matter of leaving the chicken to absorb the flavours. You could also make it with turkey. Serve with spirali.

1 tsp cayenne pepper
1¹/₂ tsp paprika
1 tsp dried thyme
1¹/₂ tsp dried oregano
1¹/₂ tsp salt
1¹/₂ tsp black pepper
450g/1lb chicken meat,
cut into bite-sized chunks

1 tbsp olive oil
1 onion, chopped
3 celery stalks, chopped
1 large green pepper, chopped
2 garlic cloves, chopped
125ml/4fl oz lager
200g/7oz can chopped tomatoes

Mix together the cayenne, paprika, thyme, oregano, salt and pepper and rub into the chicken. Leave for at least 2 hours or overnight.

Heat the oil in a heavy-based saucepan, add the chicken and cook until sealed all over. Remove the chicken from the pan. Add the onion, celery, green pepper and garlic and cook, stirring often, until softened; add another ¹/₂ tbsp of oil if necessary to prevent sticking. Return the chicken to the pan, add the lager and stir well. Cover and simmer for 15–20 minutes, until the chicken is cooked.

Stir in the tomatoes, heat through and serve on hot pasta.

MIXED SEAFOOD

If you don't like mussels or squid, you could substitute clams, peeled prawns or a firm fish such as monkfish. The main thing is not to overcook any fish or shellfish or they will toughen. Spaghetti, spaghettini or linguine are traditional for this dish, although not the easiest to eat.

450g/1lb squid, cleaned (see page 9)
900g/2lb mussels in their shells, cleaned (see page 9)
1 tbsp olive oil
1 garlic clove, sliced
700g/1½lb tomatoes, skinned, seeded (see page 9) and chopped
8 large prawns
2 tbsp finely chopped fresh parsley

Slit one side of each squid body and score the inner side with parallel lines 1cm/½in apart, then score the other way to give a cross-hatched effect. If the squid are very small you can leave them whole, otherwise cut them into chunks. Keep the tentacles in bunches, but trim off any hard parts.

Put the cleaned mussels into a large, wide saucepan. Cover with a well-fitting lid and place over a fairly high heat for 1–2 minutes or until the mussels open. Discard any mussels that remain closed, and remove and discard most of the shells. Keep the mussels in a covered bowl. Strain the liquid, leaving any grit behind, and set aside.

Heat the oil, add the garlic and tomatoes and simmer for 15–20 minutes, until thickened. Add the squid, prawns and 4 tbsp of the mussel liquid and simmer for 3–4 minutes, until the squid is just cooked. Add the mussels and heat through briefly, then serve at once on hot pasta, sprinkled with the parsley.

LIVER VENEZIANA

A satisfying, all-in-one variation on the classic. Serve with fettuccine.

2 tbsp olive oil
700g/1½lb onions, thinly sliced
600g/1¼lb calf's liver, thinly sliced
Salt and freshly ground black pepper
1 tbsp balsamic vinegar
2 tbsp finely chopped fresh parsley

Heat 1 tbsp of the oil in a heavy-based frying pan over a low heat. Add the onions, stir to coat in the oil, then cover the pan tightly so they cook in their own steam for 20–25 minutes, stirring from time to time.

Meanwhile, trim any membrane and tubes from the liver. Cut the liver into 2.5cm/1in squares.

Turn up the heat under the onions and season generously. Using a spatula, move the onions to the side of the pan. Add the remaining oil and the liver and cook, stirring frequently, for 1–2 minutes (the liver should remain pink and juicy inside). As soon as the liver is done, sprinkle in the balsamic vinegar, check the seasoning and serve at once on hot pasta, sprinkled with the parsley.

LENTIL AND SHIITAKE

Although vegetarian, this is quite a 'meaty' sauce. The lentil mixture can be prepared in advance. Serve with tagliatelle.

125g/4oz green or brown lentils
1 bay leaf
1 onion, finely chopped
1 carrot, cut into 1cm/½in dice
1 celery stalk, finely chopped
2 tbsp tamari
Salt and freshly ground black pepper
1 tbsp olive oil
1 garlic clove, crushed
125g/4oz shiitake mushrooms, sliced
2 tbsp freshly grated Parmesan cheese

Wash the lentils thoroughly. Put them in a saucepan with 700ml/24fl oz water and the bay leaf, onion, carrot and celery. Bring to the boil, then simmer for 20–30 minutes, until the lentils are soft. Mash the mixture lightly and season to taste with tamari, salt and pepper.

Heat the oil in a frying pan, add the garlic and mushrooms and sauté for 2–3 minutes. Season to taste, then stir into the lentil mixture and serve on hot pasta, sprinkled with the Parmesan.

PASTA CON LE SARDE

There are many interpretations of this unusual Sicilian dish. In some, the sardines are deep-fried, but to keep the fat content down here they are baked in the oven. Some recipes use spaghetti but this would be very difficult to eat, so I suggest penne.

12 fresh sardines, scaled and gutted
50g/2oz currants
1 fennel bulb, quartered
1 tbsp olive oil
1 onion, chopped
50g/2oz pine nuts
Salt and freshly ground black pepper

Preheat the oven to 200°C/400°F/Gas 6. Cut the heads and fins off the sardines and then cut open the belly from head to tail. Open out the flaps, backbone upwards, and press along the spine of the fish to loosen the bone. Turn the fish over and pull out the backbone. (Alternatively, ask your fishmonger to do all this.)

Soak the currants in warm water for 10 minutes, then drain and dry. Blanch the fennel in boiling water for 2 minutes, then drain and chop.

Heat the oil in a heavy-based saucepan, add the onion and cook until soft and golden. Add the fennel and cook for 5 minutes. Stir in the currants and pine nuts and cook for 2–3 minutes, then season to taste.

Toss the hot pasta with the fennel mixture and place in an ovenproof dish. Arrange the sardines on top, cover and bake in the oven for 15–20 minutes. Serve at once.

Right: Mixed Seafood

PUMPKIN WITH DATES, CHICKPEAS AND SAFFRON

The timing of this dish may vary with the type and age of the pumpkin; don't add the dates until it is nearly tender, because you want them to hold their shape. Use a pasta that will take up some of the sauce, such as radiatore or gnocchetti sardi.

1 tbsp olive oil	Good pinch of saffron
1 onion, thinly sliced	1 small pumpkin (about 700g/1½lb),
1 tsp ground ginger	peeled, seeds removed, cut into
1 tsp ground cinnamon	2.5cm/1in chunks
1 tsp ground cumin	400g/14oz can chickpeas, drained
1 tsp paprika	100g/3½oz dates, halved lengthways,
Salt and freshly ground black pepper	stones removed
350ml/12fl oz vegetable stock	2 tbsp chopped fresh parsley

Heat the oil in a large saucepan, add the onion, cover with a well-fitting lid and cook until soft, about 10 minutes. Add the spices, salt and pepper and cook for 2 minutes, stirring frequently. Add the stock and saffron, cover and simmer gently for about 20 minutes.

Add the pumpkin and simmer, uncovered, for 6–8 minutes or until the pumpkin is almost tender. Stir in the chickpeas and dates and simmer for a further 3 minutes. Serve on hot pasta, sprinkled with the parsley.

ROASTED ROOTS WITH LASSI

An earthy vegetarian dish for a winter evening. The vegetables are moistened with a mildly spiced yoghurt sauce – if you are in any doubt about the freshness of your cumin, leave it out. Serve with pasta shells or penne.

450g/1lb carrots, cut into large chunks	225g/8oz vacuum-packed or
450g/1lb celeriac, cut into large chunks	canned chestnuts
2 tbsp olive oil	Salt and freshly ground black pepper
1 tbsp light soy sauce or tamari	250g/9oz natural yoghurt
1 red onion, cut into 8 wedges	½ tsp ground cumin
225g/8oz mushrooms	2 garlic cloves, crushed

Preheat the oven to 200°C/400°F/Gas 6. Place a heavy roasting tin in the oven to heat up.

Par-boil the carrots and celeriac separately for about 1 minute, then drain well.

Mix the olive oil and soy sauce in a large bowl, add the carrots, celeriac, onion, mushrooms and chestnuts and toss to coat. Season generously, then tip into the hot roasting tin and roast for 30–40 minutes or until tender.

Mix the yoghurt with the cumin, garlic and some salt and pepper to taste. Toss the vegetables with hot pasta and spoon the yoghurt mixture over the top. Serve at once.

PAPRIKA PORK

Pork shoulder, trimmed of excess fat, gives a meltingly tender result. Serve with tagliatelle.

1 tbsp groundnut oil	2 tsp paprika, plus extra for dusting
2 onions, chopped	Salt
450g/1lb pork, cubed	200g/7oz natural yoghurt
2 tomatoes, skinned, seeded	1 tbsp poppyseeds
(see page 9) and chopped	

Heat the oil in a heavy-based saucepan over a low heat. Add the onions and cook until soft and golden. Move them to the side of the pan and add the pork. Cook, stirring often, for 5–8 minutes.

Stir in the tomatoes, paprika and a good pinch of salt. Add 125ml/4fl oz water, bring to the boil, then cover with a tightly fitting lid, reduce the heat and simmer for about 50 minutes. Add a little more water from time to time to keep the mixture moist.

When the pork is tender, remove from the heat and stir in two-thirds of the yoghurt. Serve on hot pasta tossed with the poppyseeds. Top with a spoonful of yoghurt dusted with paprika.

SAFFRON CHICKEN AND PRAWNS

Chicken, shellfish and saffron are a happy partnership. You could use cooked or uncooked prawns, in or out of their shells. Serve with spirali or casareccie.

1 tbsp olive oil	150g/5oz peas or green beans
450g/1lb chicken, cut into chunks	4 tomatoes, skinned, seeded
1 onion, chopped	(see page 9) and chopped
1 large red pepper, cut into strips	8–12 large prawns
2 garlic cloves, chopped	2 tbsp chopped fresh parsley
Good pinch of saffron strands,	Salt and freshly ground black pepper
soaked in a little warm water	½ lemon
Pinch of paprika	

Heat the oil in a deep, heavy-based frying pan, add the chicken and quickly seal all over. Remove with a slotted spoon and set aside. Add the onion, red pepper and garlic to the pan and cook until the onion is soft and golden. Stir in the chicken, saffron liquid and paprika, cover with a tightly fitting lid and cook over a low heat for 10–15 minutes, until the chicken is tender, adding a splash of water if necessary to prevent sticking.

Meanwhile, cook the peas or beans in boiling water until just tender. Drain, refresh in cold water and set aside.

When the chicken is cooked, stir in the peas or beans, tomatoes, prawns and parsley, then season generously and squeeze in some lemon juice to heighten the flavour. Heat through for a further 2–3 minutes. Toss with hot pasta and serve at once.

Right: Pumpkin with Dates, Chickpeas and Saffron

ARTICHOKES, PEAS AND PROSCIUTTO

If you can get them, use baby artichokes, quartered lengthways; you will need about 450g/1lb. Very good with casareccie.

2 small Little Gem lettuces, shredded
225g/8oz fresh or frozen shelled peas
2 small young carrots, diced
8 spring onions, chopped
2 tbsp chopped fresh parsley
Salt and freshly ground black pepper

4 tbsp stock or water
1/2 lemon
4 artichoke bottoms, trimmed (see page 9)
125g/4oz lean prosciutto, such as
Parma ham, cut into strips

Put the lettuce into a heavy-based saucepan and add the peas, carrots, spring onions, parsley, salt, pepper and stock or water. Cover with a well-fitting lid and simmer over a very low heat for about 15 minutes, until the peas and carrots are tender.

Meanwhile, bring a pan of water to the boil with the juice of the lemon and the squeezed shell, then add the artichokes and boil for 10–15 minutes, or until tender. Drain and rinse in cold water, then slice. Add the artichokes and Parma ham to the peas, heat through for about 2 minutes and serve on hot pasta.

RED MULLET WITH FENNEL AND ORANGE

Don't worry if you can't get red mullet: pale, firm-fleshed fish fillets such as sea bass or swordfish look just as good on this glowing orange sauce. Linguine or spaghetti are traditional with fish.

1 tbsp olive oil
1 onion, thinly sliced
2 garlic cloves, finely chopped
2 fennel bulbs, thinly sliced
1 tsp Pernod or a squeeze of lemon juice
Salt and freshly ground black pepper

200g/7oz canned chopped tomatoes
Grated zest and juice of 1 1/2 oranges
Good pinch of saffron strands,
soaked in a little warm water
12 black olives
450g/1lb red mullet fillets

Heat the oil in a large, heavy-based saucepan, add the onion, garlic and fennel and cook over a low heat until softened. Add the Pernod or lemon juice and season to taste.

Add the tomatoes and orange zest and juice and simmer until the fennel is just tender. Stir in the saffron liquid and olives. Lay the fish fillets on top, cover with a tightly fitting lid and leave the fish to 'steam' for 5–8 minutes, depending on its thickness. Serve at once, on hot pasta.

FRESH TUNA, RED ONION AND BALSAMIC VINEGAR

Serve this with a rocket or green salad with plenty of herbs, and use a pasta shape such as conchiglie to trap the little pieces of onion.

1 tbsp olive oil
700g/1 1/2lb red onions, diced
1–2 tbsp balsamic vinegar

Salt and freshly ground black pepper
450g/1lb fresh tuna, cut into 4 steaks

Heat the oil in a large, heavy-based saucepan over a low heat. Add the onions, stir to coat in the oil, then cover the pan tightly so they cook in their own steam for about 20 minutes, stirring from time to time to prevent sticking.

When the onions are soft, stir in the vinegar and season to taste. Move the onions to the side of the pan, add the tuna steaks and cook for about 2 minutes on each side, or until the tuna is just done. Lift the tuna out of the pan and add the hot pasta. Toss with the onion mixture, then serve at once, topped with the tuna.

STEAK, MUSHROOM AND TRUFFLE OIL

Try this as a luxurious main course with pappardelle.

1 tbsp groundnut oil
4 shallots, finely chopped
1 garlic clove, finely chopped
225g/8oz button mushrooms,
thinly sliced
Salt and freshly ground black pepper

450g/1lb beef fillet or sirloin steak,
cut into thin strips
8 tbsp beef stock
4 tbsp Madeira or dry oloroso sherry
1 tbsp chopped fresh parsley
1–2 tsp truffle oil

Heat half the oil in a frying pan and fry the shallots, garlic and mushrooms until the shallots are soft. Season to taste, then remove from the pan and keep warm.

Turn up the heat, add the remaining oil and stir-fry the steak for about 2–3 minutes. Transfer to the plate with the shallot mixture.

Add the stock and Madeira or sherry to the pan and boil until reduced by three-quarters. Return the mushroom mixture and meat to the pan and heat through briefly, then stir in the parsley and serve on hot pasta, sprinkled with a few drops of truffle oil.

Right: Artichokes, Peas and Prosciutto

MONKFISH AND ROSEMARY

Monkfish is easy to prepare and satisfying to eat. Serve with linguine.

1 tbsp olive oil	3–4 sprigs of fresh rosemary
1 onion, finely chopped	450g/1lb monkfish fillet
250ml/8fl oz tomato passata	Salt and freshly ground black pepper

Heat the oil in a saucepan, add the onion, cover with a well-fitting lid and cook until soft, about 10 minutes. Add the passata and rosemary and simmer, uncovered, for 15–20 minutes, until thickened.

Meanwhile, slice the monkfish into 'noisettes' about 2.5cm/1in thick.

Season the tomato sauce to taste, add the monkfish and simmer for about 3 minutes, until it is just tender. Serve at once on hot pasta.

VENISON, CHESTNUT AND ORANGE

Chestnuts and oranges provide a complementary flavour and help the venison to go further. Serve with bretelloni or lasagnette.

1 tbsp flour	250ml/8fl oz beef or chicken stock
Salt and freshly ground black pepper	200g/7oz canned or vacuum-packed
400g/14oz venison, diced	unsweetened chestnuts
2 tbsp olive oil	Grated zest and juice of 1 orange
2 onions, thinly sliced	2 tsp redcurrant or cranberry jelly
150ml/5fl oz red wine	

Season the flour and then toss the venison in it. Heat the oil in a heavy-based flameproof casserole and add the onions. Cook until soft, then move them to the side of the pan and add the venison. Seal the meat over a medium-high heat, then add the wine, stock and chestnuts. Bring to the boil, stirring constantly, then remove from the heat and stir in the orange zest and juice and the jelly. Cover with a tightly fitting lid and cook at a very gentle simmer for about 1 hour or until the venison is tender. Season to taste and serve on hot pasta.

VENISON, REDCURRANT AND PORT

Once the venison is minced (it is sometimes sold ready minced in supermarkets) this pasta sauce is easy to make, and it's full of traditional flavours. Serve with rigatoni.

400g/14oz venison, minced	3–4 sprigs of fresh thyme
3 shallots, finely chopped	1 bay leaf
1 tbsp olive oil	175ml/6fl oz beef stock
225g/8oz mushrooms, finely chopped	125ml/4fl oz ruby port
1 garlic clove, crushed	4 tbsp redcurrant jelly
1 tbsp soy sauce	Salt and freshly ground black pepper

Put the venison, shallots and oil in a saucepan, cover and cook, stirring occasionally, for 5 minutes. Add the mushrooms, garlic, soy sauce, thyme, bay leaf, stock and half the port and simmer gently for about 20 minutes.

Stir in the remaining port and the redcurrant jelly and simmer for 5 more minutes. Season to taste and serve on hot pasta.

LAMB WITH ROASTED VEGETABLES AND MINT

This is a great way to make a small amount of meat go a long way – and the colours are amazing. Serve with any smallish pasta – wholewheat would be good – and a glass of Sangiovese wine.

8 sprigs of fresh thyme or	2 red onions, cut into wedges
1/2 tsp dried thyme	2 yellow peppers, cut into chunks
3 garlic cloves, sliced	4 tomatoes, quartered
Coarsely ground black pepper	Bunch of fresh mint, shredded
1 1/2 tbsp olive oil	Salt
2 lamb neck fillets, trimmed of excess fat	

Rub the thyme, garlic, pepper and 1/2 tbsp of oil into the lamb. Leave for about 30 minutes, or several hours in the refrigerator.

Preheat the oven to its highest setting. Put the onion wedges in a roasting tin and sprinkle with the remaining oil. Roast in the hot oven for 20 minutes.

Shake the thyme and garlic off the lamb, reserving as much of them as you can. Sear the meat in a hot, heavy-based pan to seal on all sides. Add to the roasting tin, together with the reserved thyme and garlic, the peppers and tomatoes, and roast for 20 minutes.

Remove the lamb from the tin and leave to stand for 5 minutes, then slice and return to the roasting tin. Add the mint and the hot pasta and toss so the pasta gets the benefit of the lamb and vegetable juices. Season to taste and serve at once.

SQUID INK SAUCE

An adaptation of the Venetian dish, risotto nero, gives this dramatically dark sauce. Squid ink is sold in Italian delicatessens and some fishmonger's. Serve with spaghetti or linguine.

600g/1 1/4lb whole squid, or 450g/1lb	2 tbsp chopped fresh parsley,
cleaned squid and a sachet of squid ink	plus extra to garnish
1 1/2 tbsp olive oil	150ml/5fl oz dry white wine
3 shallots, finely chopped	150ml/5fl oz hot fish stock
1 garlic clove, finely chopped	Salt and freshly ground black pepper

Clean the squid if necessary (see page 9), keeping the ink sacs separate, and cut the bodies into strips 5mm/1/4in wide.

Heat the oil in a heavy-based saucepan and fry the shallots, garlic and parsley over a low heat until the shallots are tender. Add the squid, including the tentacles, and cook gently for 10 minutes, stirring frequently. Add the wine and simmer gently for about 25 minutes, adding the stock a little at a time to keep the mixture moist. Just before serving, stir in the squid ink to make a black sauce. Season to taste and serve on hot pasta, sprinkled with parsley.

Right: Lamb with Roasted Vegetables and Mint

LIGHT BOLOGNESE

Authentic *ragù bolognese* begins by softening the vegetables in oil and butter. We can do without the butter in this recipe, because the milk helps to give the sauce a creamy flavour. It goes with almost any pasta, from the classic spaghetti to penne or – just for fun – rotelle. Freshly grated Parmesan cheese is the traditional topping.

1 tbsp olive oil	125ml/4fl oz skimmed or
1 onion, finely chopped	semi-skimmed milk
1 carrot, finely chopped	400g/14oz can chopped tomatoes
1 celery stalk, finely chopped	200ml/7fl oz wine (red or dry white)
450g/1lb lean minced beef	2–3 sprigs of fresh thyme or
Salt and freshly ground black pepper	1 tsp dried thyme
Freshly grated nutmeg	

Heat the oil in a heavy-based saucepan, add the onion, carrot and celery, then cover and cook gently for 4–5 minutes, until soft. Add the beef, turn up the heat and break up the meat with a wooden spoon until it is no longer pink, about 2 minutes; do not overcook at this stage. Season with salt, pepper and nutmeg, then stir in the milk and cook, stirring, until it has evaporated, about 10 minutes.

Add the tomatoes, wine and thyme and simmer, uncovered, stirring from time to time, for 1–1½ hours, until thickened. Taste and adjust the seasoning. Serve with hot pasta.

BAKED MEDITERRANEAN PASTA

This vegetarian dish is a sort of cross between ratatouille and moussaka. Use penne or rigatoni – 300g/11oz should be enough for four people.

1 aubergine, cut into 2cm/³⁄4in cubes	Salt and freshly ground black pepper
1 tbsp olive oil	400g/14oz can chopped tomatoes
1 tsp coriander seeds, crushed with	150g/5oz natural yoghurt
a pestle and mortar	125g/4oz ricotta cheese
1 tsp dried thyme	½ tsp Dijon mustard
1 onion, chopped	2 egg whites
350g/12oz courgettes, sliced	
1 small red and 1 small yellow pepper,	
roughly chopped	

Preheat the oven to 180°C/350°F/Gas 4. Steam the aubergine until just tender, about 15–20 minutes.

Meanwhile, heat the oil in a heavy-based saucepan, add the coriander, thyme and onion and cook until the onion is soft. Add the courgettes and peppers, cover the pan and cook, stirring occasionally, until beginning to soften. Season generously, then stir in the aubergine and tomatoes. Mix with hot pasta and transfer to an ovenproof dish.

Mix the yoghurt with the ricotta and season to taste with salt, pepper and the mustard. Whisk the egg whites until stiff and fold into the yoghurt mixture. Spread over the vegetable mixture and bake for 30–35 minutes. Serve hot.

LAMB, APRICOT AND CHICKPEA

This Moroccan-inspired dish could be served with gnocchetti sardi, conchiglie or even couscous, which is, after all, made with durum wheat, like pasta.

1 tbsp flour	2 tsp ground cinnamon
Salt and freshly ground black pepper	1 tsp ground ginger
450g/1lb lean lamb, cubed	Pinch of cayenne pepper
1½ tbsp olive oil	200g/7oz ready-to-eat dried apricots
2 onions, finely chopped	½ x 400g/14oz can chickpeas, drained

Season the flour with salt and pepper, then toss the lamb in it and set aside. Heat the oil in a heavy-based saucepan, add the onions and spices and cook until soft and fragrant. Move them to the side of the pan and add the lamb. Cook, stirring often, to seal the meat.

Add the apricots and just enough water to cover. Bring to simmering point, then cover with a tightly fitting lid and simmer for 20–30 minutes or until the lamb is tender. Add the chickpeas and simmer for 5 minutes. Season to taste and serve on hot pasta.

HARE AND CHERRY

Like all game, hare is low in fat yet tastes rich. Depending on the size of the hare, and whether you use the saddle, legs or both, this will serve 4–6 people. If you have time to plan ahead, use the hare bones to make the stock. Serve with pappardelle.

2 tbsp olive oil	2 tbsp flour
1 onion, finely chopped	150ml/5fl oz red wine
1 celery stalk, finely chopped	1 cinnamon stick
1 hare (see above), boned and	About 250ml/8fl oz hot hare or beef stock
cut into 2cm/³⁄4in cubes	125g/4oz morello cherries in
2–3 sprigs of fresh thyme	natural juice or light syrup, drained
Salt and freshly ground black pepper	

Heat the oil in a heavy-based saucepan over a low heat, add the onion and celery and cook until soft. Turn up the heat, add the meat and brown all over. Add the thyme, salt and pepper and flour and stir for 2–3 minutes. Add the wine and cinnamon and cook over a low heat, stirring often, until nearly all the liquid has been absorbed.

Pour in enough hot stock just to cover the meat, then cover the pan and leave to simmer very gently for 1–2 hours (depending on the age of the hare), adding more stock a little at a time to keep the mixture moist.

When the hare is tender and the sauce is thick, stir in the cherries and adjust the seasoning to taste. Toss with hot pasta and serve at once.

NOTE
Cherries in natural juice can be hard to find; I used a Turkish brand of cherries in syrup with a pleasantly tart flavour. Taste the cherries before you add them; if they are too sweet, rinse them and add a squeeze of lemon juice to the sauce.

Right: Light Bolognese

PASTA AL FRESCO

Cold pasta dishes, like most other salads, should ideally be made as soon as possible before serving. Cook the pasta and drain well, then toss thoroughly with a tablespoon of olive oil and leave to cool. When cold, it is ready to use in one of the following recipes.

SMOKY AUBERGINE SAUCE

You need a gas burner for this – and you will wonder what's going on as the aubergine skin falls off in little black flakes. Don't worry – it's easy to clean up and the smoky flavour of this almost fat-free sauce is out of this world. It is good with casareccie.

2 aubergines
2 tbsp lemon juice
Salt and freshly ground black pepper
4 tbsp natural yoghurt
Good pinch of dried oregano
Good pinch of dried thyme
5–6 tbsp finely chopped fresh parsley

Place the aubergines directly on the gas burners and 'roast' over the flames for 5–10 minutes, turning frequently (use spoons), until soft. Leave until cool enough to handle, then scrape off the burnt skin. Cut the stem end off, then chop and mash the aubergines to a rough purée. Add the lemon juice, salt and plenty of pepper.

Mix the yoghurt, oregano and thyme, season to taste and then mix with the aubergine purée. Finally, mix with the parsley and cold pasta.

SALMON BLOODY MARY

Serve this alcoholic salad as a first course to kick start the tastebuds (using about 225g/8oz pasta for four people). Choose radiatore, rotelle or fusilli bucati.

50ml/2fl oz vodka
200ml/7fl oz tomato passata
2–3 tsp Worcestershire sauce
Dash or two of Tabasco sauce
Juice of 1/2–1 lemon
Celery salt and freshly ground black pepper
225g/8oz smoked salmon,
cut into thin strips
4 leafy tops of celery stalks, to garnish

Mix the vodka and passata with the smaller amounts of Worcestershire and Tabasco sauces and lemon juice. Season with celery salt and pepper, then taste and adjust the seasonings.

Stir in the smoked salmon and cold pasta and serve each portion garnished with a small stick of leafy celery.

TURKEY AND TARRAGON WITH POMEGRANATE SEEDS

Here's a special way to brighten up leftover turkey. Serve with mixed green and white fusilli.

250g/9oz natural yoghurt
50g/2oz walnuts, finely chopped
1 garlic clove, crushed
4 sprigs of fresh tarragon, leaves stripped and finely chopped
1 tsp wholegrain mustard
Salt and freshly ground black pepper
450g/1lb cooked turkey, cut into slivers
1 pomegranate

Stir together the yoghurt, walnuts, garlic, tarragon and mustard. Season to taste, then stir in the turkey.

Cut the pomegranate in half and separate the jewel-like seeds from the bitter white membrane.

Serve the turkey salad on a bed of cold pasta and scatter the pomegranate seeds over the top.

THAI-STYLE CHICKEN SALAD

Thai noodle salads are traditionally made with wiry soya bean flour noodles called *wun sen*. Vermicelli or capelli d'angelo would be the closest wheat flour alternative. In Thailand these salads are often numbingly hot with chillies – use the smaller amount unless you have built up your chilli tolerance level.

250g/9oz chicken, minced
2 tbsp Thai fish sauce
2 tbsp fresh lime juice
1–2 small fresh chillies, finely chopped, or 1/2–1 tbsp sweet chilli sauce
1 tsp soft brown sugar
5cm/2in piece of fresh ginger, finely shredded
1 small mango or papaya, peeled and cubed
8 drained canned waterchestnuts, cubed
Large handful of fresh basil leaves
Large handful of fresh coriander leaves
Large handful of fresh mint leaves
4 large Cos or iceberg lettuce leaves

Heat a wok or heavy-based sauté pan over a medium-high heat. Add the chicken, fish sauce, lime juice, chillies and sugar and cook, stirring to break up the meat, for 8–10 minutes or until the chicken is cooked. Leave to cool.

Stir in the ginger, fruit and waterchestnuts, then taste and add more fish sauce, lime juice or sugar as required.

Mix with the herbs and cold pasta, then pile the mixture on to the lettuce leaves and serve at once.

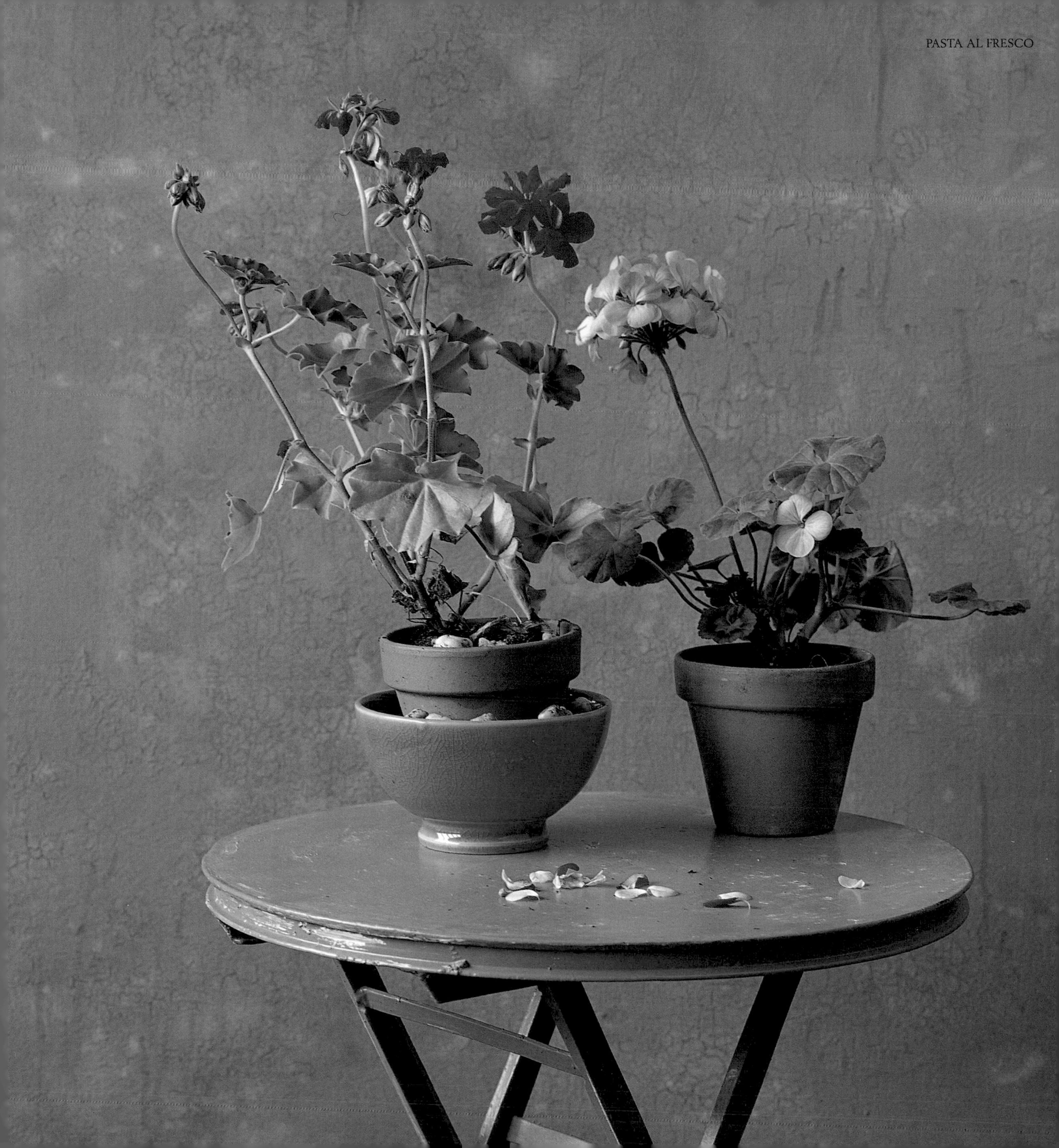

FRESH HERB SAUCE

The glorious emerald green of this sauce tells you it's packed with vitamins and minerals. Serve with conchiglie.

1 tbsp fresh tarragon leaves
4 tbsp fresh parsley
2 tbsp roughly chopped fresh chives
30g/generous 1oz watercress
100ml/3¹/₂fl oz vegetable stock

¹/₂ avocado
85g/3oz natural yoghurt
Salt
2 tbsp chopped pistachio nuts

Put the herbs, stock, avocado and yoghurt into a blender and blend until smooth. Add salt to taste.

Toss with cold pasta and sprinkle with the chopped pistachios.

HUMMUS, RED PEPPER AND OLIVE

This is lovely served on a bed of rocket – or serve a big green herb salad and a tomato and basil salad alongside it. Fusilli would be a good choice of pasta.

200g/7oz hummus
1–2 tbsp lemon juice
1 large red pepper, roasted, skinned
(see page 9) and cut into strips

4 tbsp sliced green olives
Salt and freshly ground black pepper
2 tbsp chopped fresh parsley

Mix the hummus with 1 tbsp of the lemon juice, then taste and add more lemon if necessary. Stir in all the remaining ingredients, together with the cold pasta.

SMOKED TROUT AND DILL

Palest pink with flecks of green; a pretty pasta salad that would look good with farfalle.

225g/8oz smoked trout, cut into strips
Juice of ¹/₂ lemon
2 tbsp chopped fresh dill

Salt and freshly ground black pepper
400g/14oz fromage frais
1 tsp wholegrain mustard

Put the smoked trout in a large bowl and add a good squeeze of lemon juice plus the dill, salt and pepper. Gently stir in the fromage frais and mustard, together with the cold pasta.

CAULIFLOWER, RED PEPPER, BLACK OLIVE AND FETA

This tasty variation on a Greek salad makes a main course for four but would go further if served as a first course or accompaniment. Use a spinach pasta, such as fusilli or orecchiette.

¹/₂ cauliflower, cut into florets
1 tbsp olive oil
2 tsp lemon juice
Salt and freshly ground black pepper
2 spring onions, finely chopped
2 red peppers, roasted, skinned
(see page 9) and cut into strips

4 tomatoes, skinned, seeded
(see page 9) and diced
100g/3¹/₂oz feta cheese, crumbled
85g/3oz black olives, pitted and halved

Blanch the cauliflower in boiling water for 2–3 minutes, then drain and rinse in cold water. Drain well and mix with the olive oil, lemon juice, salt, pepper and spring onions.

Stir in the remaining ingredients and toss with cold pasta.

PRAWNS AND ASPARAGUS IN LIGHT PESTO

A light, luxury-class first-course salad. Choose pasta shells or fusilli. For additional flavour, you could use the asparagus cooking water to cook the pasta.

175g/6oz asparagus tips
4–6 tsp pesto sauce
4–6 tbsp natural yoghurt

175g/6oz cooked tiger prawns or
large Mediterranean prawns

Cook the asparagus in a large pan of boiling water for 2–3 minutes, until just tender. Drain, refresh in cold water and drain thoroughly. Cut into 2.5cm/1in lengths on the diagonal.

Mix the pesto with the yoghurt. Stir in the cold pasta, then gently mix in the prawns and asparagus. Serve at once.

Right: Fresh Herb Sauce

ROASTED PEPPERS WITH ANCHOVIES AND OLIVES

The Italian job: classic, simple, vibrantly coloured and flavoured. Serve with penne.

2 red, 2 yellow and 2 green peppers, roasted, skinned (see page 9) and cut into 1cm/¹/₂in strips
2 x 50g/2oz cans anchovy fillets, rinsed (see page 7)

85g/3oz black olives, pitted
Salt and freshly ground black pepper
2 tablespooons chopped fresh parsley

Put the pepper strips into a bowl together with their juices, then add the anchovies and olives. Toss with cold pasta, season to taste and sprinkle with the parsley.

AUBERGINE AND TOMATO SALSA WITH PINE NUTS

Salting and steaming the aubergines make them meltingly tender without the need for oil. The vegetables and nuts would nestle perfectly inside conchiglie.

2 aubergines, cut into 1cm/¹/₂in cubes
Salt and freshly ground black pepper
900g/2lb ripe tomatoes, cut into 1cm/¹/₂in cubes
1 red onion, finely chopped

2 garlic cloves, chopped
50g/2oz pine nuts, toasted
Large bunch of fresh basil, roughly chopped
4 tbsp finely chopped fresh parsley
1 tsp sugar (optional)

Put the aubergine cubes in a colander and sprinkle with plenty of salt. Leave for 20–30 minutes. Rinse the aubergine well, pat dry on kitchen paper and return to the colander or place in a steamer. Cover and steam for 15–20 minutes or until tender. Leave to cool.

In a large bowl, gently mix the aubergines with the remaining ingredients, adding sugar, salt and pepper to taste. Toss with cold pasta.

AVOCADO SALSA

This colourful salsa looks very pretty with farfalle.

5 tomatoes, seeded and diced
Bunch of spring onions, finely sliced
2 garlic cloves, finely chopped
Handful of fresh coriander, roughly chopped

Dash of Tabasco sauce
3 avocados, peeled, stoned and cut into 1cm/¹/₂in dice
Juice of 2 limes
Salt and freshly ground black pepper

Mix the tomatoes, spring onions, garlic, coriander and Tabasco together. Gently toss the avocados with the lime juice, salt and pepper, then combine with the tomato mixture and cold pasta.

GREEN BEANS WITH ROASTED TOMATO AND BASIL SAUCE

Serve this simple salad with grilled fish or meat, or as part of a buffet with other salads. Penne rigate would be the pasta of choice.

1 tsp olive oil
5 tomatoes
4 garlic cloves, unpeeled
350g/12oz green beans
Salt and freshly ground black pepper

A handful of fresh basil leaves, finely shredded
¹/₂ small red onion, very thinly sliced
A few sprigs of fresh basil, to garnish

Preheat the oven to 200°C/400°F/Gas 6. Brush the oil over a baking sheet, add the whole tomatoes and garlic cloves and roast for 20–30 minutes, until the tomatoes begin to shrivel.

Meanwhile, cook the green beans in boiling water until just tender, then drain and refresh in cold water. Drain well and cut diagonally into 4cm/1¹/₂in lengths.

Rub the tomatoes and garlic through a sieve over a large bowl. Season to taste and stir in the shredded basil. Toss with the beans, onion and cold pasta and serve garnished with sprigs of basil.

Right: Roasted Peppers with Anchovies and Olives

PASTA NIÇOISE

A classic main-course salad for a summer day. The green beans look best with penne or a similarly shaped pasta.

350g/12oz green beans
200g/7oz can tuna in brine, well drained
125g/4oz natural yoghurt
1 garlic clove, crushed
1/2 red and 1/2 green pepper,
cut into 1cm/1/2in squares
1/2 tbsp capers, drained (optional)

Salt and freshly ground black pepper
85g/3oz black olives
50g/2oz anchovy fillets, rinsed
and dried (see page 7)
4 hard-boiled eggs, halved
4 tomatoes, quartered

Cook the green beans in boiling water until just tender, then drain and refresh in cold water. Drain well.

Mix the tuna with the yoghurt, garlic, diced peppers and capers, if using. Season to taste.

Mix the beans with cold pasta and the olives, then season to taste. Arrange on a plate and spoon the tuna mixture into the centre. Arrange the anchovies over the salad, and the eggs and tomatoes around the outside of the plate.

MILDLY CURRIED CHICKEN

Cordon Bleu cooks of the old school will be up in arms at the liberties I have taken with Coronation chicken. However, the original was a very rich dish and is seldom seen these days, while this revival is light and fun to eat. Fusilli would be a good choice of pasta.

1 small chicken, quartered
1 tbsp groundnut oil
1 onion, finely chopped
1 dessert apple, cored, peeled and diced
1 tbsp mild curry paste

3 tbsp mango chutney
6 tbsp natural yoghurt
2 tbsp sultanas
Freshly ground black pepper

TO GARNISH:
2 tbsp flaked almonds, toasted
Pinch of paprika

2 tbsp roughly chopped fresh coriander

Put the chicken pieces into a saucepan, add just enough water to cover, then bring to the boil, cover and simmer for 20–30 minutes, until cooked. Leave to cool in the liquid, then lift out the chicken and cut the meat into slivers.

Heat the oil in a saucepan, add the onion and apple and cook until soft. Stir in the curry paste and 150ml/5fl oz of the chicken cooking liquid and simmer for 2 minutes. Purée with the mango chutney until smooth, adding a little more chicken stock if necessary. Leave to cool in a bowl.

Stir in the yoghurt, chicken, sultanas and cold pasta, then season with pepper. Sprinkle with the flaked almonds, dust with paprika and garnish with the coriander.

CHARGRILLED SALMON WITH OLIVE SALSA

This is a main-course salad (it could be served hot or cold) full of bold flavours. If, despite careful turning, the salmon skin detaches itself, don't worry – cut it into strips and scatter over the salmon to get the benefit of the smoky flavour. Try this with spaghetti, or with radiatore or fusilli.

A little olive oil for brushing
4 x 150g/5oz salmon fillets
with skin, scaled

4 sprigs of fresh coriander, to garnish
1 lime, cut into wedges, to garnish

FOR THE OLIVE SALSA:
85g/3oz black olives, pitted
and finely chopped
85g/3oz green olives, pitted
and finely chopped
1 fresh chilli, finely chopped

4 large tomatoes, skinned, seeded
(see page 9) and diced
3 tbsp chopped fresh coriander
Juice of 1 lime
Salt and freshly ground black pepper

Mix together all the ingredients for the salsa, seasoning to taste.

Heat a ridged chargrilling pan until very hot. Brush with oil, add the salmon, skin-side down, and cook for 2–3 minutes. Turn carefully and cook the other side for 1–2 minutes. (Cook the salmon for longer if you like; these timings set up a contrast between the blackened outside and a pink, almost raw centre.) Season to taste.

To serve, spoon the salsa on to a bed of cold pasta. Add a salmon fillet, skin-side up. Top with a sprig of coriander and serve with a lime wedge to squeeze over the salmon.

Right: Pasta Niçoise

RECIPE INDEX

ACKNOWLEDGEMENTS

I would like to thank Susan Haynes and Laura Washburn for all their support and good humour. Laura had a hand in making this book look so good, too, for which I am also very grateful to Emma, Robin and Roisin.

For nurturing my tastebuds and letting me into their kitchens at an early age I bless Grandma and thank my parents. For being there for me, caring, sharing friends come no better than Helen Roylance, and I also thank her husband, Paul Brown, for that manly shoulder. Ian Chilvers has kept my spirits up with a constant stream of presents, and inspiration and recipes have been generously given by Julia Gregory, Lydia Roberts and Robert Saxton. Above all, for their kind and practical help in the kitchen, the market and the ideas department, I thank Andrew Thompson (without whom this book would not have happened) and his father, Tommy.

Text copyright © Weidenfeld & Nicolson 1999
Photographs © Robin Matthews

First published in 1999 by
George Weidenfeld and Nicolson Limited
The Orion Publishing Group
Orion House
5 Upper St. Martin's Lane
London WC2H 9EA

British Library Cataloguing-in-Publication Data
A catalogue record for this book is available from the British Library

ISBN 0297 82512 7

Stylist: Roisin Nield
Home Economist: Emma Patmore

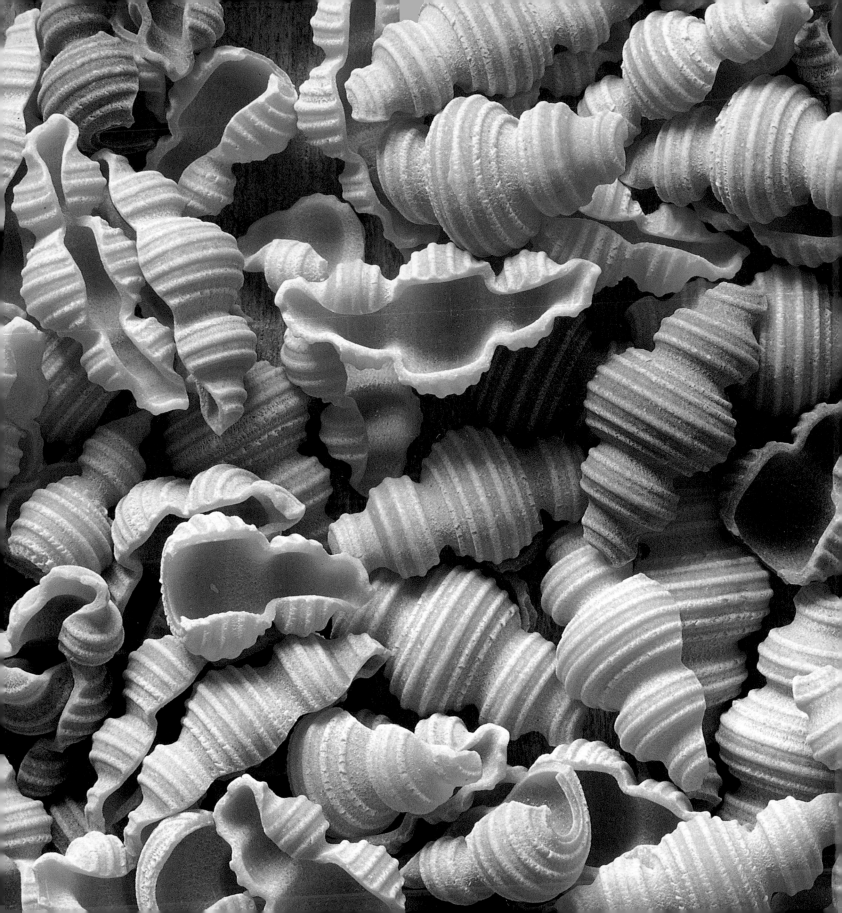